P9-CEA-428

Praise for
The 60-Minute Money Workout

"Ellie Kay has the unique ability to make mastering your family's finances easy, accessible, and yes, even fun! Written with the true insight of someone who's been there, *The 60-Minute Money Workout* is a serious finance guide that doesn't take itself too seriously...and offers something for every member of the family, even the kids."

> —TANYA RIVERO, anchor of ABC News NOW's "Good Money"

"Ellie Kay has a unique gift of being able to communicate through many mediums. She is an expert on practical money matters. This book is filled with insights and tools to help any family experience financial freedom and contentment."

> —RON BLUE, founder, Ronald Blue & Co.: Wisdom for Wealth. For Life.

"Ellie Kay is wise, articulate, and practical. Her new insights in *The 60-Minute Money Workout* are no exception. If your finances feel out of control, this book will whip you into shape!"

> —DR. KEVIN LEMAN, author of *Have a New Kid by Friday* and *Have a New You by Friday*

Praise for
Ellie Kay

"Ellie's work, helping us be better stewards, is one of the great services to families across our nation."

> —DENNIS RAINEY, executive director and radio host of *FamilyLife Today*

"The debt mentality in our society is rampant, and people are desperate. Ellie hits the nail on the head by defining those struggles and offering practical solutions in a remarkably clear way."

—HOWARD DAYTON, CEO, Crown Financial Ministries

"Ellie is amazing! I don't think she ever sleeps! She provides great information and is always a fun guest on the show."

—BILL GRIFFETH, host of CNBC's *Power Lunch*

"A splendid example of the far-reaching and positive impact that an individual with vision and faith can make in our world. Thank God for people like her who are a tremendous inspiration!"

—DR. ROBERT H. SCHULLER, The Crystal Cathedral
and television host of *Hour of Power*

The

60
Minute

Money
Workout

☑ Warm Up (Prep for Your Money Workout)
☑ Strength Training (Set Financial Goals)
☑ Cardio Burn (Put Goals into Action)
☑ Heart Rate (Measure Financial Performance)
☑ Cool Down (Reward Yourself)

An Easy Step-by-Step Guide
to Getting Your Finances into Shape

The

√ 60
Minute
Money
Workout

☑ Warm Up (Prep for Your Money Workout)
☑ Strength Training (Set Financial Goals)
☑ Cardio Burn (Put Goals into Action)
☑ Heart Rate (Measure Financial Performance)
☑ Cool Down (Reward Yourself)

ELLIE KAY

America's Family Financial Expert®

Author of *The Little Book of Big Savings*

WATERBROOK
PRESS

THE 60-MINUTE MONEY WORKOUT
PUBLISHED BY WATERBROOK PRESS
12265 Oracle Boulevard, Suite 200
Colorado Springs, Colorado 80921

Details in some anecdotes and stories have been changed to protect the identities of the persons involved.

ISBN 978-0-307-44603-9
ISBN 978-0-307-44604-6 (electronic)

Cover design by Kelly Howard

The 10/10/80 Rule™, the Cha Ching Factor™, and the Living R.I.C.H.™ Principle are trademarks of Ellie Kay & Company, LLC.

Published in the United States by WaterBrook Multnomah, an imprint of the Crown Publishing Group, a division of Random House Inc., New York.

WATERBROOK and its deer colophon are registered trademarks of Random House Inc.

Library of Congress Cataloging-in-Publication Data
Kay, Ellie.
   The 60-minute money workout / Ellie Kay.—1st ed.
      p. cm.
   Includes bibliographical references and index.
   ISBN 978-0-307-44603-9 (alk. paper)—ISBN 978-0-307-44604-6 (electronic) 1. Finance, Personal. 2. Saving and investment. 3. Consumer education. I. Title. II. Title: Sixty minute money workout.
   HG179.K3784 2010
   332.024—dc22

                              2010027095

Printed in the United States of America
2010—First Edition

10 9 8 7 6 5 4 3 2 1

SPECIAL SALES
Most WaterBrook Multnomah books are available at special quantity discounts when purchased in bulk by corporations, organizations, and special-interest groups. Custom imprinting or excerpting can also be done to fit special needs. For information, please e-mail SpecialMarkets@WaterBrook Multnomah.com or call 1-800-603-705

To the World's Greatest Fighter Pilot

Contents

Introduction

Sixty minutes a week can completely revolutionize your finances.

One hour a week. That is sixty minutes out of 10,080; 1/168th of your time.

Whether you make $15,000, $50,000, or $500,000 per year, there's one thing all of us have in common: each of us has sixty minutes per hour.

Time.

It's the great equalizer. The president's proportion equals the paparazzi's.

The plumber and the philanthropist.

The mom and the maniac.

The student and the senior citizen.

To some, the minutes fly by. To others, they drag.

For some, time is money. For others, money is time.

Nonetheless, time is the great equalizer, and all of us have the same amount. How is it that some people can milk the most out of every moment while others inanely waste eons of instants? It's what you do with time that makes it count.

The difference in how you use the resource of time lies in how purposeful you are with your hours each week. If money matters are cited as the number-one problem in most families, then it seems that they should get at least an hour of our time each week.

Give your finances sixty minutes a week and see how all things money-related will change:

- You'll get out of debt and be able to save for your kids' college tuition.
- You'll have more meaningful and debt-free vacations.

- You'll be able to figure out how to pay cash for your cars.
- You'll make a life-and-death difference around the world in the way you give money to others.
- You'll find peace with your mate.
- You'll discover contentment with your current circumstances.
- You'll latch on to hope for your financial future.
- Your money life will be completely revolutionized.

Do these promises sound like glib guarantees made from a woman with an overactive imagination and too much caffeine? Don't be fooled. These are the assurances from a woman who has been able to deliver on every single principle while financially supporting seven children on an average family income of $55,000 a year. This book doesn't promise empty theories that are written from a glass penthouse with a fine city view. No, this book was birthed among the grit and grime of having too much month at the end of the money.

My husband and I discovered early in our marriage, when we carried the heavy burden of $40,000 in debt and no hope in sight, that one hour a week could change our financial lives forever. We started these weekly money workouts, and within two and a half years—on a military man's salary—we were completely out of consumer debt, we began to pay cash for our cars, we took great vacations, we started a retirement fund, we put away money for the kids' college, and we began to support orphans in third-world countries. Well into our second decade of marriage, we began to make more money—but the one-hour workouts continued because we wanted to keep progressing in a purposeful approach to how we managed money.

Something to keep in mind during these workouts will be that you must first know your money personality so you can understand how it impacts the way you view, interact, spend, and handle money. Thus the money personality profile in chapter 2 will be a critical aspect of how each workout will function for you throughout the rest of the book.

Each chapter begins with a fun preworkout test that will ask specific questions to help you prepare to get the most out of the chapter. The work-out plans are straightforward and fairly simple. They get more compli-cated when you bring baggage to the table. So this book will show you how to check your gear at the door.

The chapters also have very specific guidelines with notes on how to target each workout and get the most out of your hour every week. What you don't cover in one workout, you table for the next one, and yet you will experience significant progress with each workout. Preparation is part of the key to success in these workouts, so I have included a list of what you will need before you begin (simple items such as a timer, paper, key resources for each subject, etc.). Each workout is tailored to a specific goal or topic.

At the end of each chapter you will find a tip sheet to use during the workout hour. This tip sheet serves as an overview to the more detailed concepts addressed in the chapter and is designed to facilitate the work-out. It will keep the action moving and alleviate any anxiety you may feel, such as, How do I remember what I'm supposed to cover?

Every money workout you do will make you financially stronger, smarter, and sweeter. You'll become *stronger,* because knowledge is power and you are practically working out that knowledge into a purposeful plan for your life. You'll be *smarter,* because any man or woman of wealth or influence will tell you that it's smart to follow the money trail—especially your own. Finally, you will be *sweeter,* because by following the guidelines for these workouts, you are forced to bind the jerk within and release your gentleperson. The result is someone who can talk about money calmly, rationally, and purposefully so that you can have a completely revolution-ized money life after only one hour a week.

1

60 Minutes to Financial Freedom

Thirty years.

That's how long it took to achieve the dream.

When I was at the ripe old age of ten, my parents won a trip to Germany because my dad bought a certain number of air conditioners for his part-time building business. They promised to bring me back "something special." I imagined a Bavarian costume, a crown that belonged to a real princess, or maybe even a china teacup. Instead, they brought me a book and a rock. The rock came from the lake where King Ludwig allegedly killed himself, and the book was a compilation of his castles and treasures. They were a little odd, but those gifts ended up serving me well.

At school, I used the book to write a report on King Ludwig that earned an A+. And the rock inspired a dream to one day see Neuschwanstein, also known as "the Disneyland Castle."

Three decades later I was able to fulfill those travel dreams, thanks to my international work with military families. As I walked through the castle's gilded hall, my imagination wandered to what life must have been like for people such as King Ludwig, who had only known a life of wealth and privilege, then to have that life cut short through suicide or murder. I decided that my life as a mother of seven wasn't that bad after all. I may not have been at the pinnacle of wealth and privilege, but I was fulfilling my dream, which also happened to be squarely in the path of another of my dreams: helping military families achieve *their* financial dreams.

Along the road to a dream fulfilled, there was hope deferred, justice denied, and paradise lost. But one thing remained true: there was a plan and purpose for the ten-year-old version of me, and my dreams—some material, some personal, and some spiritual—were worth keeping.

What were some of your childhood dreams?

Do you still dream, or did you stop dreaming a long time ago?

Would I trade my dream trip to see Neuschwanstein for anything else? Of course I would! There are boatloads of things in life that carry far greater value than a trip: my husband, kids, friends, health, and an entire host of far more meaningful things than the material ones. But the point is that if we are purposeful, principled, and proactive about money matters, then we can still hang on to those longtime dreams and watch them come to pass.

Maybe your dream is to stop fighting about money with your mate.

Maybe you want to buy a home or go to Paris.

You might dream of putting your babies through college without a mountain of student-loan debt.

Or you might want to be able to sponsor a third-world child and give her a life she couldn't have without your help.

While many people know they need to be proactive about money matters, few know the secret to putting feet to fiscal concepts. Knowledge alone is not enough to make a difference in a person's financial picture. This knowledge has to be put into action regularly in order to reach your goals.

So move over money "makeovers," it's time for the money *workout*.

Makeovers fall short of truly revitalizing your financial picture. While they address the problem and suggest solutions, implementing those concepts on a day-to-day basis can feel like driving a Honda when you were dreaming of a roadster. Another challenge of a makeover is that you don't know how to do it on your own after the experts leave.

But my money workout method will teach you how to have self-sufficiency once this book is closed.

Maybe you've tried to work on money issues but instead ended up fighting with your spouse. It might be that the thought of sitting down with all your bills is so overwhelming that it falls into the realm of impossible. Maybe you're convinced that you will never get out of debt, live in financial harmony, or own a home. It's not about how much time you spend working on money issues; it's about the quality of that time. So let's get started with your own money workout.

It's time to do our first preworkout quiz. It will only take ten minutes. The quizzes throughout this book serve to prepare you for the main workout, and you'll get a lot more out of your sixty-minute money workout if you take the time to prepare. While our dream quiz seems to be a lifestyle quiz rather than a money quiz, it's important to understand that almost every area of our lives is impacted by some financially related area. For example, an educational goal or dream coming true is often related to a work ethic, which is a financial skill. Personal goals that deal with family, marriage, and kids are definitely related to finances because of the impact that money matters have on families. Spiritual goals highly influence us in the way we use or view money. So try to fill out these dreams with that financial element in mind, and you'll get more out of the quiz. Once you've finished this exercise, it will help you focus on past dreams or expectations, current realities, and future possibilities.

Preworkout Quiz

1. What are some dreams you had as a much younger version of yourself? List a dream for each category:
   Personal

Professional

Spiritual

Material

Educational

2. If you were to rank these "dreams come true" from 1 to 10, with 1 meaning that it did not get fulfilled in any way and 10 meaning it came to pass as you dreamed it or better, then how would you rank the dreams in question 1?

    For example, maybe you always wanted a bachelor's degree from the University of Southern California; instead you earned a master's from the University of Texas. If you are satisfied with the fact that you received a better degree from a different college, you could indicate a 10 for that dream. Or maybe you always wanted to be a pilot in the air force but didn't have the requisite eyesight. So you got rated in a Cessna and went on to have a fulfilling career in real estate. You might give that dream a 5. This is your test. Although it's subjective, it represents your life and your level of contentment with your dreams.

3. Go back and add up your dream scores from questions 1 and 2.

4. Repeat the exercise, but instead of listing childhood dreams, list your current *financial* dreams for your future and/or your family's. For example, buying a house, helping third-world children, putting your kids through college with minimal debt, building an adequate retirement fund, going to Paris, having a zero balance on all your credit cards, being in a position to help others in need. You get the idea.

5. If you can, put a "dreams come true" ranking next to your current dreams using the same scale as in question 2, but base it on how likely you think it is that your current dreams will come true.

Quiz Results

In step 3, you added your scores for the dreams of your youth. See below to determine where you are with those.

25 points or less: You've had a severely average life as opposed to the life you dreamed of having as a child. Or maybe you just had a very creative imagination and dreamed of becoming a dinosaur—talk about an impossible dream (unless you're an archaeologist and you dig up dinosaurs, thus finding fulfillment by working in the same category of that childhood dream).

Another interpretation of this score can indicate an absence of exposure to key elements in your life. For example, maybe your family didn't value education, so you didn't have educational dreams. Consequently, you've either had to made adjustments and become a better person in the process of some dream-shattering realities, or you may have given up on the whole idea of dreaming and emptied your pockets of hope.

26–35 points: Either you weren't very imaginative as a child and didn't daydream about life in the future, or you had an above average culmination of your dreams coming true. This score could also indicate that you were purposeful and realistic in ways to make your dreams come true, even though you fell short of the youthful version of yourself. It might be that you've had some challenging life-changing events, but you've recovered from them enough to be able to take the second chance this world has given you.

36–45 points: You might be a lot like my husband, Bob, whose dad took him to a Blue Angels airshow when he was a child. After the show Bob told his dad, "When I grow up I want to fly those jets with the funny noses." He grew up to fly the F-4 Phantom, the same jet he saw at the airshow. You have had most of your dreams come true and/or you've been very satisfied with a different interpretation of your childhood dream. Even if your real dream came true almost exactly the way you imagined it, you still may not be content, because contentment is often a choice. But it appears you have had every opportunity to be satisfied with the results of your childhood dreams.

45–50 points: You might be one of those people we know as someone who is "living the dream." You were prescient or intuitive as a child, and it seems you followed your passions to see these dreams to fulfillment. Very few people can say that they've had most of their dreams come true, but you are one of that minority. With great privilege comes great responsibility, so you are now in a position to help others set goals and make their dreams come true. You can't do everything for others, but you can help and give them hope. Congratulations on living the dream.

In step 5, you were to rank how likely you believe your new dreams will come true. This exercise measures the realistic nature of your goals and expectations as well as your optimism about your future. So add up those results and then go back and read the result descriptions above to see what areas may need to be adjusted in order to set yourself up for success in your financial life.

Boundaries for the 60-Minute Money Workout

As we prepare for the workout, it's important to establish boundaries and do a little mental preparation as well. Some of the workouts in this book will be done alone, but other chapters will involve your mate, an accountability partner, or your family. The guidelines, however, are the same whether there's one or ten people involved. Here are some boundaries to keep in mind:

No condescension or negativity. Don't talk down to anyone who's involved in the process, and if you're alone, do not allow your mind to entertain any negative self-talk. It doesn't matter if you've failed in the past, lack knowledge about certain aspects of finances, or have a bad self-image. For one hour, you are going to be focused on learning, keeping a positive mind-set, and making progress in the workout. In fact, that's why it's called a "workout," because you are working out some of these things in your life to have a positive result.

No interrupting others when they are talking. If you have trouble with interrupting others, then sit on your hands. It will serve as a reminder that you are to listen in an active manner and not spend the time thinking about what you're going to say next. If sitting on your hands fails to keep you from interrupting, then get a tennis ball and pass it back and forth. If the ball isn't in your hands, then your lips should be still. And if you are talking and the other person starts to interrupt, just wave the ball and smile.

No name-calling. For one hour you are going to be part of the southern genteel class, an aristocrat born and bred with good manners. For a measly hour, you're going to say nice things and not throw around labels.

No throwing food. Okay, this may seem like a funny and random boundary—it is. During my husband's military service, a formal dinner could turn into a food fight if one wayward roll got out of control. So if you are prone to this kind of behavior, then maybe you shouldn't do your money workouts over a meal.

If you truly have a problem with throwing golf clubs or Scrabble boards when you are frustrated, then you will need to do your money workouts with another mature person (or couple) or even a professional counselor.

Begin each workout by saying one positive thing. Most of us have negative self-talk tapes that run through our heads, and sometimes we just need to destroy those. *I haven't ever been able to stick to a budget. You're such an idiot, how can you possibly get it together at your age?* These are trash-talk negative statements that should be thrown out. Instead, tell yourself something positive about yourself. Or tell your partner one positive thing that you like about him or her. It will be more beneficial if these positive things are financially related, such as, "You have a good work ethic" or "You really saved a lot when you bought that new notebook after shopping around."

End each workout by saying one positive thing. You started on a positive note, and now you're going to end on a positive note. If your positive statement can relate to the workout, that would be ideal. For example, "I didn't quit. I stayed and finished the entire thing." Or if you're talking to another family member, "You really did a great job of listening, and I appreciate that you didn't interrupt."

Create an environment that encourages comfort and success. If you hate Mondays, then maybe you shouldn't make Monday your money workout day. You want your workout to be set up for success, which means you should do it at a time when you feel rested, the kids are not underfoot, and you are in a place that is conducive to conversation. Part of this boundary point is to put this money workout on your calendar at a time and in a place that promotes a relaxed yet purposeful atmosphere.

Gather workout folders. One major positive about these money workouts is that you don't have to purchase any journals, financial kits, or other expensive materials to make this work for you. The basic supplies you need are minimal and inexpensive. You will need to invest in a dozen pocket folders from a local office supply store (less than $10) and label them for the different workouts. For example, if you are working on a spending plan, then when you are finished for the hour, you can place the notes you made into the folder and later easily pick up where you left off.

Keeping your working materials separate also allows you to put other related materials into the folders and keep them organized, which makes your workouts easier. For example, if there's a new Web site you want to check out for "The 60-Minute Travel and Fun Guide Workout," then throw it into the appropriate pocket folder, and you'll have it at the ready when you need it. If you have a college scholarship application you want to help your student complete, then place it in "The 60-Minute College Plan Workout" folder. This is all very low tech and simple.

Have a timer on hand. You need to stick to the times listed, even if you're "on a roll" and want to keep going beyond the hour. Do *not* go overtime.

It's the same as a too-long workout at the beginning of a physical fitness routine. An extended workout will do you in and make you sore the next day, and a workout marathon defeats the purpose of the exercise. If your "money talks" have an established start time and a set finish time, they are going to be a lot less painful. Realize that you won't get all the problems solved in just one hour. That's okay. You still will make progress in that hour. Then you can come back to it and either make a little more progress or finish it. Part of the benefit of *The 60-Minute Money Workout* is that you'll make the best, most productive use of those sixty minutes. A set hour is a wonderful motivation to stay on topic and move through each section quickly, without getting bogged down by any of the negatives listed above in the boundaries section. The regular part of the workout will keep you busy enough, because there's no time for squabbling, condescension, or negativity.

The 60-Minute Money Workout

This is how the sixty-minute money workout works: every chapter has a different goal for the workout, such as retirement planning, vacation trips, or paying down consumer debt. You will have a timer and specific materials for each workout (such as calculators, Internet access, bills, etc.). The prep work for each exercise will list the materials you need. At the end of each chapter, you will find a tip sheet that will serve as an outline when you have the weekly topical workouts.

As with a physical workout, the keys to your success are consistency and intensity. For this workout to facilitate the miraculous in your life and revolutionize your finances, you have to practice it regularly (at least once a week) and you have to abide by the boundaries. So let's get started.

Pick the goal you want to work on. Then grab a timer. You can set it for one hour and watch the time for each section. Or you can set the timer for the minutes available in each section, and when it goes off, it's time to move on to the next section.

Here is how the times are broken down and what you do within each section.

1. Make-Up-Your-Mind Warmup (5 minutes)

This part of the exercise is listed in the boundary section as "Begin each workout by saying one positive thing." There's a proverb that says, "As a man thinks in his heart, so is he." This is where you are going to begin to get focused on good things. If you are alone, then you will begin by closing your eyes and breathing deeply to relax your body and to get rid of any distracting thoughts from a busy day. If you are in the habit of praying, this would be a good time to meditate in order to think about what you want to accomplish during the next hour.

If you are with a family member or your mate, begin by saying something positive to him. For example, you could take your spouse's hands, look into his eyes, and say something affirming. Then you will make a commitment to work on the issue in the session in order to get back into good financial shape. For example, "During this hour I want to work on a plan to have a debt-free vacation for our family."

2. Strength Training (10 minutes)

It usually takes more than one mistake or circumstance to get into financial trouble. Whether you are working out alone or with someone else, you need to realize that this is the part of the workout where you move from being a victim of your choices or circumstances to taking the necessary steps toward having victory over them.

While step 1 was to start with affirming words and a commitment to work on your money topic, this section is a time to write down your goals so that you will have a tangible and objective standard to work toward. This gives both of you a temporary focus for today and a long-term focus for the next few months, as well as a big-picture view for the future.

Your goals will depend on your topic of the day. For example, if you are discussing a budget, your goals might include (a) setting up a budget that is real and workable, (b) staying on that budget for the next six months in order to learn how to spend less than what you make, and (c) establishing a budget habit that is a financial vehicle that will get your family out of consumer debt, help you pay for your kids' college, and fund your retirement. Each chapter will guide you specifically through each section of the workout.

This is also the time for you to jot down any obstacles that have come up in the past and to plan how you can overcome them. For example, you may want to budget, but you keep going off budget, which is an obstacle. You could add, "Have accountability about budget" as a means of overcoming that obstacle. Or you could write, "Review budget monthly to stay on task."

3. Cardio Burn (20 minutes)

In this step, you give feet to your goals. Basically, underneath where you wrote out your goals in step 2, you will write down the steps involved in how you plan to get there from where you are now as well as delegate who is going to be responsible for what, specifically. For example, if you're setting up a budget, write down the specifics of what your budget needs to include, how you plan to implement your budget, and how often you'll check in on your progress toward this goal. This may not seem like a lot of time to do all this during this section, but realize that you may not accomplish your goal during your first workout.

You can also carry the work from this section over to the next section—if you don't have extra work to do in the next session. The key is to keep your discussion moving and to work on what you can. Whatever you don't finish, you can get to the next time around. There are tools for every chapter in the "Tool Center" link on my Web site, www.elliekay.com.

Discuss and work on a plan for your topic of the day. Yes, this section and the next are the two hardest sections, but they are also the "fat burning" phases where you get the most benefit. When you write down the step-by-step plan for your topic, make sure your approach is realistic, and be sure to give and take when it comes to discussing this topic with your mate.

If you find the discussion stalls or otherwise gets bogged down, then you may want to table a particular point and get back to it later, or you may even need to agree to disagree.

4. Take Your Heart Rate (20 minutes)

This is the point where you do any of the specific work after you've written out the step-by-step plan from the previous section. It's also a time to crunch the numbers and fill in the details (facts and figures) on any tools or work sheets you are using. For example, if you need to get the facts on your credit and debt information, this would be the time to do it. That means you may need to have a computer and Internet access. Don't worry about the specifics now; this chapter is just an overview of how the program works. Each chapter will list the specifics of what you will need to do for this section. The examples I use here are just to familiarize you with the concept.

If your topic concerns credit and debt, then this would be the time to order a free copy of your credit report at www.annualcreditreport.com. Or if the workout is about saving money, you could use this time to set up an automatic allotment from your paycheck or from your checking to savings accounts. If your plan for the day is debt reduction, you may decide to cut up all but two or three credit cards and cancel some of your open credit accounts (be sure to cancel the most recent cards first and keep the cards you've had for five years or longer in order to maintain the longevity part of your FICO—Fair Isaac credit score).

Don't procrastinate. Do this during this "work" part of the workout. This will help minimize the temptation to procrastinate on the practical aspects of your workout and also keep you on track with your goal for the day. If you don't have any outside work to do during this time, then feel free to expand your discussion from step 3 in order to reach closure on your topic of the day.

5. Congratulations Cool Down (5 minutes)

Sit back and grab a glass of something cool to drink and reflect on all you've accomplished in just one hour! You started on a positive note, and you're going to end on a positive one as well. If this is an individual workout, tell yourself something that is truthful and encouraging. For example, "I finished the first hour, and if I continue to do this workout, I will master this topic."

If you are working out with someone else, then take this time to tell your partner one thing that you appreciate about today's workout to end the discussion on a positive note. For example, you can say, "I noticed you gave my ideas a lot of respect. I appreciate that." Or, "When I got upset and started to cry, I appreciate the way you weren't condescending. Thank you."

Keep in mind that just as you don't get physically buff after one workout, your finances aren't going to be in perfect shape after this first effort either. So during this step you will set the topic and the time for your next workout. Maybe you'll have a continuation of today's workout, or maybe you'll look at a new area. Whatever the case, decide what you're going to cover next time and put it in writing. After you and your mate have exercised with this money workout a half dozen times, you'll find yourself stronger, smarter, and sweeter.

✓ Workout Tip Sheet

At the end of every chapter is a "Workout Tip Sheet" that you have on hand to help facilitate the workout and keep it flowing, without wasting time to look back and forth in the chapter. Here's a sample Workout Tip Sheet.

1. Make-Up-Your-Mind Warmup (5 minutes)
- Say something positive.
- Commit to work on the topic.

2. Strength Training (10 minutes)
- Write down realistic short-term and long-term goals.
- List means of overcoming obstacles.

3. Cardio Burn (20 minutes)
- List specific steps to accomplish each goal and delegate responsibility.
- Research topical tools at www.elliekay.com.

4. Take Your Heart Rate (20 minutes)
- Implement work on each specific step.
- Fill in facts and figures.

5. Congratulations Cool Down (5 minutes)
- Say something positive.
- Set topic for next workout.

2

The 60-Minute (Split) Personality Workout

I've always been economically tight.

From my earliest memories, I had a fascination with pennies and nickels. I learned to earn them, save them, and share them. In some ways, the paradox of being a born saver and a born giver was unique, but it was as inbred as my crooked left pinky finger (my son has the same one, as did my grandma).

Being tight was reinforced in my family.

My parents praised me when I earned it and kept it. In fact, I kept so much of the money I earned as a budding entrepreneur that my parents began to spend it for me. They sent me to Spain after the fifth grade with some of my business proceeds. They required that I buy my own lunch at school if I didn't want to brown-bag it. Then they mandated that I pay for my own auto insurance, summer camp, and clothing. All of this reinforced my "born saver" tendencies, even if the financial pressure did seem a bit excessive for a child my age. I learned from it, and yet my husband and I don't make our kids pay for these essentials while they are children. We do things differently.

On the opposite end of the spectrum, we have my husband, Bob. He was born to be wild, at least in terms of spending the money he earned. Thankfully, he had a fabulous work ethic and knew how to earn some dough by pulling weeds at the age of seven or digging ditches in his teens. He earned enough money to buy his own car, but he never kept much of a savings account.

If it's true that opposites attract, it's also true that opposites complete each other.

It only took a decade for us to realize that our different money personalities could be leveraged into an asset rather than a liability. Bob helped me live life a little fuller. I helped him plan for life in the future.

This chapter's workout is designed to reveal your money personality and/or combination of personalities. Most people have a "split personality" of two or more different money personalities. By knowing your or your family member's profile, you will be able to better understand how you and others view money, how this view impacts your finances, and how your personality causes you to interact with other family members or people in your life. This personal money profile is a critical thread that is foundational and woven throughout the rest of the workouts.

Monopoly and Your Money Personality

A simple way to determine your money profile is to observe your behavior when playing the game Monopoly. He who gathers the most money, properties, and hotels wins the game, right? When I was a child, I pretended that Monopoly money was real. Winning with $10,000 in my pile was a great feeling! Ever the born saver, I didn't risk buying properties when I didn't have a cash reserve. But sometimes I lost the game because I wouldn't spend money on properties and didn't build wealth as a result. To win at Monopoly, both born savers and born spenders need to figure out how to balance saving and spending. The same is true in the real world. We all need to balance how we can spend money to make money and yet not spend any money we don't have.

For example, a dangerous game that certain money personalities play in the real world has to do with consumer debt. There's a temptation to charge vacations, Christmas gifts, car repairs, and more as a matter of course, knowing that there isn't any real money to cover the money they've borrowed. So much of this view of money has to do with a person's basic personality.

Learning who you are in terms of your money personality will help to accept the "pros" of your money style and learn how to compensate for the "cons" that your natural tendencies emanate in the ever-elusive quest for balance. So let's get started with a preworkout quiz.

Preworkout: Fiscal Fitness Test

In the self-test below, you will find ten basic money questions. Give yourself a number ranking from 1 to 10 for each question using the following scale:

Rarely or Never	Sometimes	Frequently or Yes
1 ——————————	5 ——————————	10

1. Do you currently live on a budget?
2. Do you consistently stick to your budget?
3. Do you only buy something because you really need it? (Not just because you want it?)
4. Do you give 10 percent of your income to a nonprofit organization?
5. Do you regularly give away material possessions?
6. Do you have a total consumer debt load of less than $2,000?
7. Do you save at least 10 percent of your income?
8. Do you have a savings account with at least six months' worth of income in it?
9. Do you own a retirement account or mutual fund of any kind, including 401(k), Roth IRA, etc.?
10. Do you buy something only after comparing prices?

The result of this fiscal fitness test will let you know how you rank with regard to the financial essentials. A large part of your grade is determined by how you manage the strengths and weaknesses of your money personality.

Add up the numbers you put next to each question. After you tally your scores, take a look at your fiscal fitness level based on the following chart:

30 or less: Your grade is "Failure to Meet Standards"

You are in the "greatest need" category and have all the characteristics of a born spender who has never made any modifications in her financial habits. If you haven't yet filed for bankruptcy, it is possible you will do so within the next two years unless you change your course and set it for financial recovery. If you are in this category, I suggest you call your local consumer credit counseling agency and set up an appointment.

31–50: Your grade is "Needs Improvement"

You are below average in your savings tendencies. You likely have a large amount of credit card debt and are headed down the path of financial despondency unless you make some critical changes now.

51–70: Your grade is "Severely Average"

If you are like a typical American family, you are somewhat content with the status quo but believe your family's financial situation will somehow right itself on its own. You tend to have a lot of the characteristics of born spenders, but there is still hope for your born-saver characteristics to kick in and save the day (and the money!). You are a prime candidate to become financially healthy rather quickly if you will rise to the challenge and make the changes your family needs.

71–85: Your grade is "Above Average"

At least one of the partners in this family is likely a born saver with an ability to influence the household budget and other financial aspects in the home. This person may know many of the right things to do financially but could still lack some of the accountability to follow through in specific areas. Perhaps a specific event has derailed your finances, and you're ready to get back on track. If you make just a few modifications in your family's financial plan, you will be in a position to eventually help others who have great financial difficulties.

86–99: Your grade is "Significantly Above Average"

You have a great financial situation and outlook. However, you are in danger of falling out of balance in your financial situation if your money management skills have become an obsession or a compulsion to save and invest your money. If you are still giving away 10 percent of your income, this indicates that you are not completely out of balance. You need to be sure that you find flexibility and latitude in navigating your family's finances.

100 (or a Perfect Ten): Your grade is "Delusional"

Are you really perfect? Hmm…maybe you've deceived yourself just a bit here and there. Besides the fact that *you* could be writing this book, you need to be aware of the characteristics described in the previous paragraph. If you can honestly say that you have balance and are still generous with your money, then you might want to consider mentoring others to help them in these critical areas. However, because you think you are perfect, you may lack understanding for those who do not measure up to your standards. Finding ways to use your gifts and talents to help others can keep you humble and compassionate.

The 60-Minute (Split) Personality Workout

If you haven't done the pretest, do it now. Then you will be ready to dig in to this workout.

This money workout is one of the few exercises in the book that really should be done individually rather than with someone else. You can be in the same room with your spouse or family member, and each of you can have a book and both do the workout (setting the timer, etc.) at the same time, but you need to do the work individually rather than collectively. Yes, you may (and probably will) compare notes afterward, but it's important for you to see how you view yourself before you have someone else telling you how you should view yourself.

Now we are ready to look at what this workout entails in detail. Please don't read ahead in this chapter, because you will spend part of your sixty minutes reading about the different personalities and another part of the timed work assigning a ranking to those personalities. You don't want to jump ahead of yourself because you'll lose some of the spontaneity that is essential in getting the kind of instinctive response that might be lost if you work ahead. Read the following workout carefully, and then go straight to the "Workout Tip Sheet" at the end of the chapter, skipping over the money personalities. The workout will have you come back and read the money personality section, and you will find the workout much more genuine as a result.

1. Make-Up-Your-Mind Warmup (5 minutes)

During the warmup for this topic, it's important to start out by saying something positive about yourself. Take a few deep breaths and relax your mind and body, focusing on getting rid of the day's baggage. Pray a prayer of dedication to finding out who you really are and what makes you do the things you do.

Maybe you know that you're a born spender, and you've said a lot of negative self-talk about your personality. No longer will you listen to the same old message that says, *You can't stop spending; you'll never get it together*. Instead, you're going to say something like, *Now is the time to find out how my money personality impacts the way I do business. When I discover this, I will be able to manage financial issues better*.

Or maybe you're a born saver and can't seem to lighten up when it comes to spending what it takes to go on vacation, even if you can afford it. You may be highly critical of born spenders or intolerant of your spouse's attitude toward money matters. Instead of the old thought patterns that say, *I don't need any help;* she *needs help.* You can say something like, *I know I've found it hard to spend money, even when I have it. But today I'm going to discover my money personality, and I'm going to celebrate the good part of my discovery.*

The next element in this warmup is for you to make a conscious commitment to discover the full depth of your money personality. You may already know if you're a basic spender or saver, but there is more to it than the basics. Tell yourself that you will embrace what this exercise reveals about yourself and other family members. Rather than judge yourself or others harshly in what you discover, make the decision right now that you are going to cut yourself and others some slack. Give yourself the benefit of the doubt and believe that if you know your money style and why you view these issues the way you do, then you will be better equipped to enhance the assets of your personality and manage your weaknesses.

2. Strength Training (10 minutes)

Write down the results of the pretest and read the evaluation associated with your grade. Then read the results for the next two higher grades and see what those people are doing differently from what you are doing. Go back to the pretest and look at the areas where you are not performing up to standards. Maybe you aren't living on a budget or building a savings account. Maybe you could be more generous in your giving. List the areas where you could improve.

After you've listed these areas that need attention, make a list of ways to overcome obstacles and decide what you can do differently. Write these down on paper in order to reinforce where you have been up until now, where you want to be in the future, and how you can overcome obstacles (or excuses) with practical action.

3. Cardio Burn (20 minutes)

Go to the section titled "Money Personalities" (which you were instructed to skip earlier). As you read, next to each personality write down how you would score yourself, from 1 to 10, as to how it describes you. A 1 equals "this is not me at all," and a 10 means "this is completely me."

Now go back and take the two top personality scores to determine which money personality you are (or which combo you and your spouse are). If you have time left over in this section, you can also score what you believe to be your spouse's or other family member's money personality. Eventually, you will want to do this for every person in your family who has an impact on your finances—including your children or extended family members who might be living with you.

4. Take Your Heart Rate (20 minutes)

Some of this workout is subjective, so not everything will be laid out for you in black and white. List what you believe to be the strengths of your money personality. Then determine how to emphasize those in order to make them become an asset to your family's money matters. Next, list what you believe to be the weaknesses of your money personality. Determine how to minimize or overcome these so they are not a liability to your family's money matters. As you go through this section, think about savings, retirement, college savings, budgeting, vacations, consumer debt, and children's money issues. List the pros and cons of your money personality when it comes to managing these different areas.

If you have time, repeat this section with your partner in mind.

5. Congratulations Cool Down (5 minutes)

Say something positive about your money personality and what you have learned about yourself from this exercise. Do not dwell on your pretest grade if it is lower than you like. Instead, decide what grade you would like to have in the future, and then think about the strengths of your money personality. Set the time and topic for your next workout. You may want to devote a workout just like this one to evaluating other family members' personalities.

✓✓✓

Skip to the "Workout Tip Sheet" at the end of this chapter. The workout will have you come back and read the following section during your timed sixty minutes.

Money Personalities

I live in Southern California, where there are actors around every corner. I see them waiting tables, working in retail, and holding down temporary office jobs. When I asked Austin, an actor friend, how he gets into a character's role, he said, "The first thing you have to do is understand that character's motivation. What drives him? What makes him get up in the morning? What is the character's primary incentive?" I think we can say the same thing when we look at money personalities, because they are what motivate our attitudes toward material things, money, and work.

As you read these definitions as part of your cardio burn section, be on the lookout for characteristics that describe you, your partner, and other family members and rank them. So next to each personality, write a number from 1 to 10. One means you are nothing at all like this personality, and 10 means you're a dead ringer. Keep two things in mind as you read:

1. Although most people are a combination of these personalities, they tend to remain within the basic framework of a born spender or a born saver. A born spender is neither bad nor good, likewise a born saver. Balance is the ultimate goal.
2. Any personality can move into or out of balance at any time, which is both a word of caution and a source of hope.

At the end of this section, you will take the two personalities that ranked highest and voilà, you will have your (split) money personality. Then go back and read this section with other family members or even a friend in mind. It will help you understand why they never can seem to make ends meet or why they always try to pick up the tab or why they are not giving when you expect them to be more generous.

Power Paul

Money can be the ultimate strategic pawn in the power game. This personality is a born spender who uses money for *control* and for his or her own ultimate gain. "He who has the money makes the rules" is the basic philosophy of this style. A person who does not produce her own money independently may feel a loss of power with Power Paul. If he is the primary breadwinner, then he may use this position as a means of control to keep his partner in her place. Conversely, he can rarely handle a spouse who makes more money than he does, because she is too much of a power threat. The undiluted version of this personal money style tends to clearly dominate and

- will make all financial decisions,
- does not seek his partner's input,
- will not allow access to financial information, and
- uses these strategies to secure a position of strength in the relationship.

On the other hand, Power Pauls tend to be risktakers, the ones who are the movers and shakers in this world. If brought into balance, they can learn how to bring out the skills and talents of the people around them. A diluted version of this personality will shift some of their power to others, thereby enabling those around them to become empowered to do well for their team, their company, their families, or their communities.

Security Stephanie

Security Stephanie was raised in a family that was one step away from being homeless. This particular kind of money personality is motivated to save money by the powerful emotion of *fear*. She has memories of not knowing where her next meal was coming from and having to move from dingy apartment to dingy apartment in order to stay one step ahead of the bill collectors. She may have even had some of these experiences in adulthood, which has tainted her perspective. Consequently, she has vowed, much like Scarlett O'Hara: "I'll never go hungry again. No, nor any of my folk. If I have to lie, steal, cheat, or kill. As God is my witness, I'll never be hungry again."

Not every Security Stephanie saves money because of a background of poverty; a variety of circumstances birth this money style. Sometimes she's fearful because of a recession, political uncertainty, a sudden job loss, or a lack of education. But the common characteristic is the fear of not having enough for basic needs, retirement, the kids' college tuition, a rainy day, etc. This person may be drawn to marry someone who represents financial security. She also tends to be a born saver who always wants to add "just a little more" to her investment programs, because she feels she never has quite enough money in savings. The loss of financial security is about the worst thing that can happen to Security Stephanie. So when she says no to a family vacation, even when the funds have already been budgeted, it is her insecurity speaking.

On the upside, this money personality tends to have a great amount of compassion for others in difficult situations. As she comes into balance and learns to pry her fingers off that fistful of dollars, she can be one of the most generous money personalities because she knows what it's like to live with only a little. Stephanie needs to learn that perfect love casts out fear and that there is nothing healthy about cowering in a corner. When she learns to manage her money in balance, then she will no longer be fearful about her financial future and will have the freedom to fulfill her purpose in life.

Tightwad Timothy

Born savers have many overlapping traits and may even seem to be identical at first glance. There are shades of gray, however, that distinguish them as decidedly different. Tightwad Timothy is much like his twin sister, Security Stephanie, in that they are born savers. But Timothy doesn't save money based on a fear for security. He does it because the main characteristic of this money style is that he's *cheap*. In the golden age of Hollywood, Jack Benny forged an entire career over his shtick of being cheap. Bob Hope said, "Jack really liked my book. I know because he called me up from the library to tell me."

Tightwad Timothy is always looking for an extra buck and is more tempted to compromise his integrity in order to earn that buck. We could even call Tightwad Timothy a "Shifty Steve" because this money style may battle a selfish drive to save a buck anywhere and everywhere—even at the expense of others or his own integrity. Am I saying that all Tightwad Timothys are dishonest? Of course not. It is simply that they are more vulnerable to these temptations because of their self-centered tendencies. An undiluted version of this personality is also stingy with his time, talents, food, material goods, and even candy. (Don't even think about asking them to share their chocolate!)

On the upside, this personality does a bang-up job at stretching his company's resources, cost cutting in a fat budget, and doing more with less. He has an innate ability to see where you can cut corners if you're not that concerned with quality. When brought into balance, however, a Tightwad Timothy can do what seems like the miraculous in a community project and in making a positive impact with available resources.

A good exercise for balance is for Timothy to begin giving away 10 percent of his income on a regular basis. If he has a bad attitude about it, he will not find any satisfaction in giving. But if he can develop a good attitude about it, he'll find more freedom in his life and be well on his way toward balance.

Worrywart William

The interesting thing about Worrywart William is that he can be either a saver or a spender—he's one of the few money styles that can shift either way. This person is obsessed with money *worry.* He talks about it, thinks about it, makes decisions based on it, and even dreams about it. He can have too little and worry about how he is going to pay the bills, send his kids to college, and fund his retirement. Or if he has more money, then he worries about losing it, other people wanting it, making bad decisions with it, or loaning it out to those who will not pay it back.

He worries about whether he will get a raise at work and whether the lawn boy will ask him for a raise. He stresses over where he will vacation and if a natural disaster will cut his vacation short. He frets over whether he will have a job next year or whether he can handle the additional responsibility should he get his dream promotion. He squirms about whether to pick up the tab when out with friends or whether they will pick up the tab.

He needs to learn about mind over matter. If you don't mind, it doesn't matter! But he seems to mind about everything financial. He is obsessed with the thought of money, work, material goods, and anything related to financial issues. It seems like he worries for pleasure.

The good news for a Worrywart William is that most of the things he worries about will never come to pass. When a bit of balance arrives at this money personality's front step, and he finally chooses to open the door, then he is the kind of person who can be the most grateful of any money personality for life's simple pleasures. He also is more likely to appreciate contentment when he chooses to eliminate the extremes of his concentrated personality. He has worried away more hours than his peers, and if the worse should happen, he's already got the worrying part behind him!

Spendthrift Sarah

Spendthrift Sarah never lets her money see the inside of her pocket. A spendthrift is born to *spend uncontrollably,* and she is truly bothered by having extra money. This money style will oftentimes spend the birthday money, the annual bonus, and even an inheritance well before she ever receives the first nickel! No one knows if spendthrifts are motivated by a sense of responsibility toward disposable income or if they view all income as disposable. Her brain does not engage when it comes to spending. This personality is so rudimentary, they're almost like toddlers. When they go shopping, they have a toddler's tendencies:

- If I like it, it's mine.
- If it's in my hand, it's mine.
- If I can take it from you, it's mine.
- If I had it a little while ago, it's mine.
- If it's mine, it must never appear to be yours in any way.
- If it looks just like mine, it's mine.
- If I think it's mine, it's mine.
- If I can't pay for it, it's still mine—because I have credit.

Debt is a major by-product of the spendthrift's makeup, and even if she is able to manage her debt load, she doesn't manage to set aside much for a rainy day. Sometimes she tells herself she's spending for others—the kids, her friends, her family—but she's not, because she's just spending, and that's only an excuse. When a Spendthrift Sarah wins a sweepstakes, inherits property, or hits the lottery, she spends it all within two years. If she leverages the equity in her home with a home equity line of credit or a second mortgage, she usually spends that within a year to eighteen months.

This personality needs the balance of a patient born saver who can teach Sarah how to stop her spendthrift ways and teach her the difference between wants and needs. On the upside, when Spendthrift Sarah finally learns the value of living within her means, she can become a supersaver as she learns to shop for sales, combine savings factors with online purchases, and stop shopping when she reaches her budgeted limit. These personalities tend to be high energy and very creative. When they put that creativity toward saving money and living within their means, they become an asset to their families and their communities.

Feel-Good Francine

Feel-Good Francine's motto is "I feel, therefore I shop." Her spending is determined by her *emotions*. She hits the mall whenever she feels sad, lonely, angry, or even when she feels good and wants to celebrate. She uses shopping as "therapy." During our time in the military, I knew more than a few Feel-Gooders who added a new piece of furniture, bought a new car, or remodeled the bathroom when their spouse was deployed out of country. Impulse buying is a common characteristic of someone who is spurred to buy consumer goods based on her emotions. Of all the personalities, the compulsive shopper who obsessively buys more and more to deal with negative feelings is the most likely personality to need professional counseling to overcome this emotion-based response to money.

Feel-Good Francines need to find another outlet for their feelings, which will then bring them into balance. When people with this personality start their own businesses and put their energy into something productive, they often succeed, because building an income makes them feel as good or better than they felt when they were spending money. But if they don't deal with the root cause of their emotional response to money matters, then they might destroy everything they have built in their families' finances, their home-based businesses, or even in their work outside the home. With accountability and counseling, Feel-Good Francines can become overcomers who help others overcome their feelings-based approach to finances.

Love-Ya Laura

Aunt Laura may look a lot like her sister, Aunt Francine, because they are both materialistic. She knows the latest designers, whether your purse is a knockoff, and which styles are from last season. The difference is that Francine uses her money to feel good about herself, but Aunt Laura uses her money to make *others feel good about her.* Forget the Beatles' song, Love-Ya Laura believes that money *can* buy you love!

Those who practice this money style use money as a substitute for love and time. If she works extra long hours to please her boss, then she buys toys to make it up to her kids. If she goes into debt to get her husband that TAG Heuer watch he has always wanted, then she believes he will never stop loving her. While some look at Lauras as irresponsible, a closer look sees a person who is crying out for love. This personality knows no distinction between male and female. They can as easily be a Love-Ya Louie as a Love-Ya Laura. Rather than being admirable, they're pitiable, because they will never know if people love them for who they are or just because they're picking up the tab.

People with this personality often find themselves divorced, with "money matters" cited as the reason. Patient spouses will understand the root cause for this dysfunctional spending and will help Love-Ya Louies and Lauras to understand that they are loved for who they are, not what they can buy. When Love-Yas turn their focus away from loving through spending and allow the balance to come into their personalities, then they have the capacity to be great philanthropists who learn to give of themselves. They will be able to give their time out of the abundance of their love for others rather than out of a need to give in order to get. Unconditional love for Lauras and Louies can help them come into balance and can yield a harvest of their newfound ability to offer unconditional love to their families, community, and the world.

Balanced Brian

Just as the scales of justice are blind and perfectly in balance, this personality is blind to extremes. A Balanced Brian is so perfect it makes you sick! Balanced Brian has just the right combination of strengths from all of these money styles. He understands what is truly important in life and tries to be generous with his resources while still maintaining an aggressive savings style. Brian realizes that his kids won't just catch good habits, he has to teach them well, and he knows that his money cannot buy their love. Brian is in balance right now—but he wasn't always. He used to have debt problems and may have even fallen prey to some compulsive expenses that nearly ruined the family's budget. But he found his feet and he found balance.

Balanced Brian also realizes there are no guarantees that the future will be trouble free; he knows that Power Paul's idea of ultimate control is only an illusion. So he's thankful that through diligence, his finances and perspective on money are currently in balance. Just like a watchman on a wall, he is constantly looking for those distractions that can attack his family's finances and tries to address negative attitudes and unrealistic expectations before they become a problem.

Keep in mind that all these money personalities, in their undiluted and imbalanced versions, are extreme examples. The final personality—Balanced Brian—is the balance we want to achieve. It is a personality that may have been either a born spender or a born saver, but he has found a way to leverage his strengths while managing his weaknesses.

The point to these personality profiles is that people tend to move in and out of them on a regular basis, but they tend to remain within the basic categories as a born spender or born saver. Feel-Good Francine at her extreme is just as close to the center point as Tightwad Timothy is on his end of the spectrum. Born savers tend to believe that their personality is "right" or "best." But if you look at the undiluted versions of extreme born savers, you will see that they are not balanced. So no matter what your predominant money personality, you can move toward balance, and it will make you stronger, smarter, and sweeter.

☑ *The 60-Minute*
     (Split) Personality
Workout Tip Sheet*

*If you haven't taken the pretest, then do it before you start this workout.

1. Make-Up-Your-Mind Warmup (5 minutes)
- Say something positive.
- Commit to discovering your money personality.

2. Strength Training (10 minutes)
- Write down the results of the pretest.
- List the means of overcoming any obstacles listed on the pretest.

3. Cardio Burn (20 minutes)
- Read the money personalities and score them.
- Determine the results of which money personality you are (or which combo you and your spouse are).

4. Take Your Heart Rate (20 minutes)
- List the strengths of your money personality and ways to emphasize them.
- List the weaknesses of your money personality and ways to minimize them.

5. Congratulations Cool Down (5 minutes)
- Say something positive about your money personality.
- Set the time and topic for your next workout.

3

The 60-Minute Spending Plan Workout

For two decades, I've called my husband "the World's Greatest Fighter Pilot." Once when I went into the squadron to take him lunch, I asked the operations officer to page "the World's Greatest Fighter Pilot." To my amazement, the entire squadron showed up! Yes, you can tell a fighter pilot, but you can't tell him much. Take, for instance, the idea that he should stick to flying jets instead of trying home repairs. One of the things he's fond of saying is, "A man's got to know his limitations." I'll remind him of this when he wants to remodel the kitchen himself or replace the tile flooring by his lonesome. No, he can do it all—just ask him. When we were stationed in Spain, we once had a problem with the electricity in our apartment. Call an electrician? No. Why would you do that when you have a fighter pilot in residence? The story ended with a six-floor building in complete darkness.

The good news about Bob is that when it came to budgeting, he began to realize he was a born spender and I was a born saver, and maybe, just maybe, he needed a little help in sticking to a spending plan. Thankfully, we were doing our money workouts and worked on our spending plan together. It was instrumental in helping us achieve our financial goals, including getting out of consumer debt and paying cash for our cars. This was part of our "dreams come true," and we were grateful to have a plan.

Many of the dreams Americans have can be related to their finances:

becoming debt free, paying cash for cars, owning their own home, putting their kids through college, or taking a nice vacation. Maybe you discovered this in the first chapter when you did the pretest. With *The 60-Minute Money Workout*, you can begin to accomplish these dreams by starting with a spending plan, also known as a budget. During the next workout, we're going to look at my 10/10/80 Rule™, which outlines a spending plan that is both practical and effective. If you are married, it is important to do this workout together. You can each do the pretest by yourselves, but you should do the workout together.

This workout is probably going to be one that you repeat from time to time. Many of the other workouts will also bring you back to this one. For example, when you look at the workout for chapter 6, "The 60-Minute Cha Ching Guide to Paying Less Workout," it will impact the numbers on your spending plan by reducing what you spend so you can increase the money you put toward a savings or retirement account. When you do the debt workout, as you pay off your credit cards, you'll tweak the numbers on your spending plan. When you learn how to save money and reduce your liabilities, whether you cut your food budget or reduce your insurance premiums, the results will have a significant impact on your spending plan.

Therefore it's critical to view your spending plan as an organic mechanism, something that will change from quarter to quarter, month to month, and maybe even from week to week. If you were to compare this workout to a physical workout, then this would be your primary cardio. Whether you normally walk, swim, spin, or play tennis—it's what keeps your heart healthy.

But first things first. Before we do the workout, it's time to do the pretest.

Keeping your money personality in mind (from the previous chapter), review this pretest and check which statements are mostly true for your situation. In taking five minutes to do this test, you are thinking about the reasons or excuses that may be limiting your ability to either establish a spending plan or stick to one. After you answer true or false for the following statements, go back and look at the statements again, marking *R* for a reason and *E* for an excuse. This is a subjective test, and it is *your* answer that matters.

Preworkout Test

Why I Cannot Stick to a Spending Plan

- My spouse bought that new _____, and that is why we're in financial trouble.
- My parents have tons of money. They could help us, but they won't.
- Our [neighbors, parents, siblings, friends, etc.] have financial difficulties, and it's just the way life is for most people.
- My spouse is a spender, and I have no hope of financial recovery as long as we're married to each other.
- My spouse was laid off from his job, and we can't even pay our bills. I'm so angry at [the company, the economy, the president, God, _____].
- A family member has been hospitalized with a severe medical problem, and we can't pay our bills.
- We work hard for our money and end up paying too much money in taxes. It isn't fair!
- The cost of living is so high where we live, we'll never get ahead.
- My spouse made a bad investment, and my children and I have to pay the price for this mismanagement.
- My former spouse has lots of money, but I have to work day and night to make ends meet. I don't deserve this!
- I couldn't afford to go to college, so now I'm stuck in a dead-end job.
- I have a college education, but I'm overqualified and underpaid for this job.
- We've tried different spending plans, but they don't work for us because we can't stick to them.

- We've read a lot of financial books, but none of them have worked for us.
- We've talked to a financial counselor, but that didn't work for us.
- We have a reason why everything you've written in this book won't work for us.
- We're not to blame.

60-Minute Spending Plan Workout

This section is a detailed version of the spending plan workout with the 10/10/80 Rule Spending Plan Resource Sheet included in the following "Take Your Heart Rate" section. The tip sheet is included at the end of the chapter for your convenience. Don't forget to set the timer for each section. When the timer goes off, move to the next section whether you are finished or not. You will make progress, and next time you can work on what you don't finish this time.

1. Make-Up-Your-Mind Warmup (5 minutes)

Look at your pretest and think of something positive to say about your results. It may be the statements that you did not check, such as, "At least I don't blame my parents for my financial difficulties," or "I'm thankful that I'm not married to a born spender." If you are doing this with your spouse, then say something positive to him or her as well. Then commit to putting together (or revising) your spending plan.

2. Strength Training (10 minutes)

Look again at your pretest results and the statements you checked that apply to your spending plan and/or financial attitude. Take all the *E*'s (excuses) and write them on a piece of paper. Determine which excuses could be related to your money personality and how they can be brought into balance to get rid of the excuses. It's important to be honest with yourself and with your spouse if you are doing this with him or her.

Once you've completed that list, tear up that sheet of paper.

It's time to eliminate those excuses, because you are through with excuses. Now you will be able to establish and stick to a successful spending plan, which will change your life for the better!

3. Cardio Burn (20 minutes)

Keep your money personality in mind (and your spouse's if you are working together). Then work through the following six steps.

- **Set Goals**. If you don't know where your family finances are going, how can you reach your desired destination? Goals are a road map to where you want to be. For example, you want to set up a plan to pay off consumer debt or save for a house or establish a college fund for baby Sweetpea.

- **Determine Your Current Spending.** Part of the preparation work for this exercise is to gather your bills or bank statements so that you can write down everything you have spent over the last three months. If you spent cash, write down what it was for. This will help you discover how and where you are currently spending your money.

- **Determine Your Current Budget**. Take the information from the previous step and put it into a budget chart to determine your current spending based on your present spending habits. Or you can use the budget tool at www.elliekay.com for both the current spending and the new spending plan you are establishing. You will be able to recognize the excess right away and see what your problem areas are.

- **Create a New Budget.** Now that you've seen where all the money has been going, it's time to fill out the new budget based on your new goals. You will do this in detail in the next part of the money workout ("Take Your Heart Rate") with the 10/10/80 Rule.

- **Measure Your Progress.** Continue to keep records, and at least once a quarter, redo this workout so you can measure your progress toward your financial goals. Are you paying down debt? Are you breaking in the new "cash or debit instead of credit" habit? Are you building your savings accounts? During these workouts, you may need to reassess either your goals or your spending plan.

- **Reward Yourself!** Your budgeting efforts should be a combination of hard work and fun, so create a reward system that accompanies each of the financial goals you have set for your family. You might want to build a splurge fund into your budget.

4. Take Your Heart Rate (20 minutes)

This is where you list your new spending plan in great detail. It should follow the 10/10/80 Rule in order to be successful:

- 10 percent: Share with a nonprofit organization, such as your church or a third-world relief effort;
- 10 percent: Save through an allotment or designation to a savings account and for investments;
- 80 percent: Spend wisely by following some of the tips listed later in this book.

Be sure that you set the timer for this section. If you've never established a spending plan before, you will not be able to finish this in an hour. That is okay. Just record how far you've come today and then pick it up again the next time you work out. The secret is to make progress, not solve all your budget problems in the first hour.

5. Congratulations Cool Down (5 minutes)

Say something positive about the hard work you did today as well as a positive proclamation for the future. Set the topic for your next workout. If you did not complete the spending plan, then set it as the topic for the next workout and do it no later than seven days after this first effort. Put the new date on your calendar. You will have a plan in place soon, and it will make all the difference!

10/10/80 Rule™ Monthly Spending Plan Resource Sheet

Account Name	Current Spending	New Spending Plan
Tithes/contributions (10%)	_____	_____
Savings (10%)	_____	_____
Clothing/Dry Cleaning (5%)	_____	_____
Education/Misc. (5%)	_____	_____
Food (10%)	_____	_____
Housing/Utilities/Taxes (30%)	_____	_____
Insurance (5%)	_____	_____
Medical/Dental (4%)	_____	_____
Recreation/Vacation Gifts/Christmas (6%)	_____	_____
Transportation (15%)	_____	_____
Totals		

☑ The 60-Minute Spending Plan Workout Tip Sheet

1. Make-Up-Your-Mind Warmup (5 minutes)

- Say something positive about the results of the pretest or otherwise.
- Commit to establishing a workable spending plan.

2. Strength Training (10 minutes)

- Write down the results of the pretest.
- List a means of overcoming the obstacles indicated on the pretest.
- Take the excuses and tear them up.

3. Cardio Burn (20 minutes)

- Reread the detailed notes on this section as necessary.
- Determine your previous spending plan or spending amounts and fill in the chart using past bank statements or bills.
- Follow the six steps to create a workable spending plan, working on the specific step that applies to where you are in the chapter.

4. Take Your Heart Rate (20 minutes)

- Fill in the detailed 10/10/80 Rule Monthly Spending Plan.

5. Congratulations Cool Down (5 minutes)

- Say something positive about your progress today and/or your spouse.
- Set the time and topic for your next workout.

The 60-Minute Retirement and Savings Plan Workout

I have the greatest respect for mothers of young children, especially those who have more than one preschooler at a time. When Jonathan and Joshua, our two youngest, were only two and three, we nicknamed them "Senior Mischief and his Protégé." If they disappeared for more than ten minutes at a time, or if they were quiet in the next room, then it spelled *trouble* with a capital *T*. One day when I was in the laundry room, they got into some *T* in the time that it took me to move one load from the washer to the dryer and turn it on. By the time I returned to the kitchen, they had removed the child safety locks from the refrigerator. They stood giggling and pouring milk over a pile of cracked eggs on the floor. Jonathan said they were "helping Mama make a cake." Whoever came up with the saying, "There's no use crying over spilled milk," never had preschoolers!

Today, a lot of people are in capital-*T* trouble because of what the stock market, the real estate market, and unemployment have done to their nest eggs.

One of the areas hardest hit is savings and retirement, and the spilled milk in this case is the economy. We can't control it, and it seems to want to ruin us! When the economy goes south, your employer stops matching your 401(k), your bills are harder to pay, or something happens financially to make saving or investing a lot more difficult, it's important that you do not further deteriorate your retirement by stopping your contributions to savings. If you don't continue to participate, no matter what the economy, no matter what the matching portion, you risk destroying your future retirement as well as your rainy-day savings.

This chapter's workout is about continuing to keep savings as a priority while you work through various economic difficulties. The worst money move you can make is to stop saving, or if you're not saving, the worst money move would be to not get started at all.

The information on how to cut back on spending so that you can save more is in chapter 6, "The 60-Minute Cha Ching Guide to Paying Less Workout." But in this chapter, you're going to define some of the retirement and savings plans that will work best for your finances.

Preworkout Test

Answer true or false for each statement.

1. I have less than $2,000 in consumer debt (credit card or installment loans for items such as appliances, furniture, or other depreciating material goods).

2. I am single and have one years' worth of living expenses in my savings account; or

    I am married, and we have one income and eight to ten months' worth of living expenses in a savings account; or

    I am married, and we have two incomes and six to eight months' worth of living expenses in a savings account.

3. I currently contribute the maximum matched amount to my 401(k); or

    I am married and my spouse currently contributes the maximum matched amount to her 401(k).

4. I either pay cash for my cars or I buy a car with no more than a twenty-four-month loan.
5. I have a child, and I have started a college fund to which I contribute at least $50 per month.
6. I do not have a home equity line of credit (HELOC) or a second mortgage on my home.
7. I have fully funded either a Roth IRA or a regular IRA each year for the last three years.

Test Results

For whatever you cannot answer true to, as it applies to your case, you will need to do "The 60-Minute Savings and Retirement Plan Workout" so that you *can* answer true. If you answered false to most of your questions, here is the order of how you should do the workouts:

- Debt repayment (see chapter 5, "The 60-Minute Debt Workout")
- Regular savings account
- 401(k) funding
- Cash for cars
- College funding
- HELOC or second mortgage repayment (see chapter 5, "The 60-Minute Debt Workout")
- Roth IRA or regular IRA funding
- Investing

Please note that some of these categories overlap. For example, some college funding information is included in the investment chapter, and funding a 401(k) is not only retirement but also certainly an investment. As a rule of good financial management, you should not start investing in the stock market until you have already funded the categories listed before it. This pretest determines which workout you will do for "The 60-Minute Retirement and Savings Plan Workout."

Read the appropriate category prior to the workout so you will know what you need to bring to the table for this workout to be effective.

The 60-Minute Retirement and Savings Plan Workout

1. Make-Up-Your-Mind Warmup (5 minutes)

Take a good look at where you are on the pretest. Maybe you are at the very beginning and need to start to build a basic savings account. Take a few deep breaths and give yourself permission to "start where you are and do what you can." Do not be discouraged by what you don't have or that the economy has taken so much of your nest egg. Instead, say something positive to yourself about the results of the pretest, and if you are doing this workout with your spouse, then remember the boundaries and guidelines from chapter 1 and say something positive to your spouse.

Make a commitment to have a successful workout. Remember that *success* simply means that you make progress and get through the entire hour of the workout. It doesn't mean that you have to get your entire savings strategy in place today; it just means that you do some work on it. What you don't finish today, you'll finish in the next workout.

2. Strength Training (10 minutes)

Write down the results of the pretest and use that to decide the topic of this workout (savings accounts, 401(k) savings, college funding, IRAs, or other investing). Follow the order in which the items appear on that list and what you've accomplished in the workout pocket folder that you've labeled "The 60-Minute Retirement and Savings Plan Workout." You may have an urge to work ahead on this list and that is fine, but only after you've done the workouts for the prioritized items beforehand. For example, you want to look at college investing but don't have an adequate savings account. Do the savings workout first and so on, building up to the college funding workout. That way, you are very much aware of what insufficiencies you still have in your overall savings and retirement portfolio, even as you begin to plan for college costs.

List the means of overcoming obstacles that have prevented you from succeeding in this area in the past. For example, maybe you've never had an automatic allotment for 10 percent of your paycheck to go into savings, and you end up spending all your paycheck. That is an obstacle, and setting up an automatic deduction is a way to overcome that obstacle. Another common obstacle is that both spouses have different priorities. You may want to prioritize saving, and your spouse may want to take a nicer family vacation instead. This is definitely an obstacle that you can work to overcome. Another possibility is that you run out of money. You can't save what you don't have, which is an obstacle indeed. One way to overcome this obstacle is to increase your income (see chapter 12, "The 60-Minute Launch Your Home-Based Business Workout"). A second way to overcome this is to reduce your committed expenses (see chapter 6, "The 60-Minute Cha Ching Guide to Paying Less Workout"). You get the idea: be honest with yourself and learn to identify and overcome obstacles during this part of the workout. Keep your work written down in the pocket folder to review when you repeat this workout in the future.

3. Cardio Burn (20 minutes)

It is time to read the detailed notes on your chosen section. The various sections are listed after this detailed workout. If you are working out with someone else, read it out loud so it will be fresh. Stop and clarify any concepts that are not clear so that all parties understand the information in that section. If your spouse or partner doesn't have the grasp you have of some of these concepts, this is a time to remember the boundaries (including no condescension), especially when clarifying these concepts. Think through or discuss with your mate, if you are working out in tandem, all the options that you bring up.

Determine the steps you need to take today to implement your plan and which steps you can do during the time frame allotted for the next section. Don't just discuss these, but write them down, keep them in the folder pocket, and check off each step as you accomplish it. Whether you finish a step this time or next time, all of it will eventually get done. Success is defined as getting through the hour and making progress, even if it's an inch at a time.

4. Take Your Heart Rate (20 minutes)

Go to the investment tool section of www.elliekay.com and access the tools involved with your topic of choice. Work through the tool calculators to get the information you need. Print out and keep the results of your calculations, and rework the tool for several different options (interest rates, investment amounts, etc.) depending on the saving/retirement section you are working on for this workout.

Take proactive steps to implement the plan you discussed in the previous step. This may include getting and filling out an automatic or electronic pay allotment form to start saving from your paycheck or getting information from magazines or online to accomplish your goals. Get account numbers if you need them. This part of the workout can be done in front of a computer where you can access the appropriate forms or information online and submit them. In other words, *Take action!* If you are at a place where you don't have a form, then delegate who will get the rest of the necessary information, and on the last step, set up another workout when you can then fill out the appropriate forms after you've gathered the information you may not have today.

5. Congratulations Cool Down (5 minutes)

Say something positive about your progress today and/or about your spouse. You got through the entire hour. I know you've made some kind of progress, so now is the time to congratulate yourselves! Set the time and topic for your next workout.

Resource Information for the 60-Minute Savings and Retirement Workout

Regular Savings

If you are in credit card debt, the first thing you should do with your money is pay down that debt and work through chapter 5, "The 60-Minute Debt Workout." If you've got a good interest rate on your credit card debt, then you're paying 10 percent. If you're on the higher end of the interest scale, then you could be paying 20 percent or more. There are very few sure investments that have a return of a solid 10 percent these days and fewer that show upward to 20 percent! Therefore, the best place to put any extra money is your checking account, where you'll use it to pay off those high-interest credit cards as soon as possible.

Second, it's more important, initially, to build a solid regular savings account than it is to invest in stocks and bonds. If you are a one-income family, then you should try to have eight to ten months' worth of living expenses in your savings account. If you are a dual-income family, then you should have six to eight months' worth of living expenses in your savings account. The reason is obvious: if there's only one wage earner, and he loses his job, then you will have no other source of income until one of you finds employment. If both of you are wage earners, you'll definitely feel the pinch if one of you is suddenly out of work, but at least the other person is still bringing in some money.

For a solid savings account, I like to use www.ingdirect.com because of its higher interest rates for savings and higher yields on certificates of deposit (CDs). Or you can look at the latest rates from a variety of savings institutions at www.bankrate.com.

As you are building a savings account with 10 percent of your net income, you need to keep in mind that we're still talking savings here, not investing. A savings account not only builds a buffer for the possible loss of employment, but it allows for those unexpected expenses that arise, such as a new roof, tires, braces, car repairs, fixing appliances, etc. You want to have savings so you can pay cash for these items rather than finance them. A savings account also affords you the luxury of time to seek the best buy.

A secondary motive for savings is to pay cash for consumable expenses (however you might want to define those), and entertainment. Concentrate on saving for the essential needs in order to be in a much better position to accumulate wealth and have the freedom to do some, no-kidding, real investing.

401(k)

Most everyone knows that a 401(k) savings plan is an employer-sponsored program that allows employees to contribute a portion of their salary to a retirement plan. One of the great aspects of a 401(k) is that your contribution to the plan may be partially matched by your employer. In the best-case scenario, some companies will match 100 percent, up to a preset limit. Even those employers that are cutting back to a mere 25 percent match are still an excellent deal for workers. If your 401(k) fund does not perform well in a bad economy, you still have the 25 percent return on your contributions. So don't let dwindling balances in your fund keep you from investing—especially if your employer matches your deduction in part!

Unless you're desperate and cannot contribute because of extreme financial straits, then stopping contributions to a 401(k) is a bad idea. You are not getting any younger, and each generation seems to live longer. Many estimates predict that it won't be uncommon for baby boomers to hit a hundred. Hey, if forty is the new thirty, and fifty is the new forty, then why wouldn't one hundred be the new eighty? Chances are good that you will need more money in your retirement than any generation in history because of this longevity factor. You'll still need to eat, live, and be cared for.

The other reason you want to keep contributing to a 401(k) is that you would miss the tax deferral, which is a significant benefit. If you're in the 28 percent tax bracket, and you put $10,000 in the plan, it only costs you $7,300 of actual money that you would take home.

If you don't continue to participate in your 401(k), no matter what the economy, no matter what the matching portion, then you risk deteriorating your financial future in retirement.

The bottom line is this: unless you're independently wealthy, have a rich uncle, or have some other options to fund your retirement, you'll need a fat 401(k) for your retirement years. Set this up with an automatic withdrawal from your check, and you'll never miss what you never see. Remember that pretax contributions are the fastest route to building the kind of wealth you will need in the years to come.

While there are different kinds of 401(k) plans with benefits and limitations, it is not my purpose here to take the time and space needed to cover these details. This section is designed to provide you with the information you need to start your 60-minute retirement workout. Whenever you change employers, you will need to rollover your 401(k) funds to either an individual retirement account (IRA) or the 401(k) plan offered by your new employer. Be sure that you know how long you have to be employed for your employer's matching portion of the fund to be vested. It may vest immediately (meaning it is yours and is portable for you to take with you) or you may have to be with the company for a year or more before the matching portion of the 401(k) will be yours to move to a new fund (via a transfer or a rollover). A final option would be to leave the money where it is, if your former employer allows you to do so. See the section on IRAs for help in finding a discount broker who can assist you with moving funds from your 401(k) to an IRA.

Cash for Cars

One of the major decisions Bob and I made early in our marriage that took us from a broke lifestyle into a rich lifestyle involved about two years of delayed gratification. That was more than twenty years ago, and ever since then, we've paid cash for our cars and put the amount we would have to pay in car loan interest and new car depreciation into our kids' college funds. So here's the radical statement: driving for free helped our kids go through college free.

It's all in the math. An average new car costs $26,000 and will lose at least 25 percent of its value as soon as you drive it off the lot. If you take out a car loan, your monthly payments, if you're an average American, will be $475 per month for six years or a total of $33,000 when you add up the interest. And your six-year-old car will have a cash value of $6,000. So you've lost $27,000 over the lifetime of that loan.

But look at how easy it is to turn that around. In our family, we didn't buy a second car and kept the first one until it was paid off. So we went about two and a half years being a one-car family. If you use the figures from the example above, and you set aside the monthly car payment for only ten months ($475 x 10), you'll have $4,750. Meanwhile, the current value of your car is only $2,000. But when you add the value of your car to the cash you've saved, you have a total of $6,750 to spend on a good used car. See chapter 6, "The 60-Minute Cha Ching Guide to Paying Less Workout," to find a guide on how to buy a car cheaply.

If you drive that car for only ten months, then its value should not go down and you could probably get $6,750 for it, plus you continue to set aside the $475 from the car payment you still don't have for another ten months and have another $4,750 to add to the $6,750, for a total $11,500 to upgrade to a nicer car. This can go on and on until you are basically driving your cars for free, and you can put the money you would have spent on interest and depreciation toward your children's college fund.

College Funding

This section is about setting up a college fund for your child. A fuller discussion of college funding can be found in chapter 10, "The 60-Minute College Plan Workout," which discusses creative ways to fund college, find scholarships, and look for other funding options. This workout is about saving money for college, and it is as individualized as your dreams. College aspirations vary from family to family and even from child to child. Your options will vary based on such factors as your income, the number of children you have, and the number of years between now and when a child starts college. Here's a guide to the most popular investment tools:

- **UGMA (Uniform Gifts to Minors Act).** Parents of young children can start saving now for education in a tax-smart way. By investing in a UGMA in a child's name, the earnings are taxed at the child's marginal tax bracket rather than the parents'. The account, however, must be registered in the child's name. An adult (usually a parent or grandparent) serves as custodian and is responsible for investing and managing the assets. But the child is the "beneficial owner," meaning that the assets belong to the child and no one else. At age eighteen (in most states), control of the assets must be turned over to the child (which could be a disadvantage for this plan when it comes to financial aid qualifications). All states offer UGMAs, and many have adopted the Uniform Transfers to Minors Act (UTMA) as well. An UGMA allows children to own stocks, bonds, mutual funds, and other securities, but an UTMA allows the children to also own real estate. Under UTMA, parents can delay giving the assets to the child until age twenty-one.

  For example, if your bouncing, beautiful, three-year-old daughter has interest income of $700, the annual federal tax on that is zero. If she has income of $1,400, $700 is taxed at a rate of 10 percent ($70). By comparison, if you are in the 28 percent bracket in 2011, the tax on the $1,400 total would be around $400. By having the fund in your daughter's name, she's just saved an additional $330 for her college education.

- **U.S. EE Savings Bonds.** If income from these bonds is used to pay for education expenses, any earned interest may be excluded from taxes. But this exclusion is phased out beyond certain income levels.

- **Zero Coupon Bonds.** The interest on these bonds is deferred until they mature, when it is paid in a lump sum. Parents have to pay income tax on interest as it accrues each year the bond is held. It's often wise to ladder these bonds, where the bonds come to maturity in each year of the child's college career.
- **529 Plan.** This is an education savings plan operated by a state or educational institution, designed to help families set aside funds for future college costs. As long as the plan satisfies a few basic requirements, federal tax laws provide special tax benefits to you, the plan participant (see Section 529 of the Internal Revenue Service at www.irs.gov). These 529 plans are usually categorized as either prepaid or savings, although some have elements of both. Every state offers a 529 plan, and it's up to each state to decide what it will look like. Educational institutions offer a 529 prepaid plan but not a 529 savings plan (the private college independent 529 plan is the only institution-sponsored 529 plan thus far). At www.finaid.org you can review your state's plan, but parents can invest in any state's plan, no matter where they live. And regardless of what plan you choose, the beneficiary can attend any college or university in the country. What's more, grandparents or other benefactors can contribute money to a 529 plan. However, these contributions may limit a child's ability to qualify for financial aid in the future. It is important to review the state ratings for residents and nonresidents, as some are rated better than others. These plans are growing in popularity, and it is projected that there will be a total of $175 billion to $250 billion invested in 10 million to 15 million accounts by the year 2011.
- **Coverdell Education Savings Accounts (ESA).** The Coverdell ESA allows up to $2,000 of pretaxed income to be invested annually toward a child's education. This is dependent upon

your modified adjusted gross income being less than $95,000 as a single tax filer or $190,000 to $220,000 as a married couple filing jointly in the tax year in which the money is contributed. The $2,000 contribution limit is gradually reduced if the modified adjusted gross income exceeds these limits. There is also a requirement that the funds must be spent before the child turns thirty. This education IRA will not interfere with the parents' ability to invest in a tax-deferred annuity in their own retirement account, but it will count heavily against the student when financial aid packages are calculated.

Because Coverdell IRA funds can be rolled over into a 529 without penalty, parents can sidestep its principal drawbacks— the age limit and the fact that the IRA counts as the child's asset, which can adversely affect his or her ability to receive need-based loans. Therefore, a Coverdell account may be the best single investment option for parents whose annual income is less than $50,000. The accounts are easier and less expensive to set up than 529 plans, and people in this lower tax bracket aren't usually able to take advantage of the maximum lifetime contributions mandated under a 529, which range from $110,000 to $305,000, because they don't pay that much tax in the first place.

- **Prepaid Tuition Plans**. An individual state or educational institution may offer a 529 prepaid plan that is similar to a 529 plan but less risky. These prepaid plans allow parents to pay tomorrow's expenses at today's prices either by the year or by the credit hour. The drawbacks are that even though parents can often transfer some of the plan's funds to other state colleges or private tuitions, those schools do not guarantee the same services and prices. Thus college students could come up short. Contributions to prepaid plans might also reduce a student's eligibility for financial aid on a dollar-to-dollar basis, which is more of a penalty than the student would face with a 529 savings plan. If the child does not attend college, the contributions are refundable, but there might be a cancellation fee and/or loss of interest earned.

It's important to compare 529 plans to find the plan that works best for your family. Visit www.savingforcollege.com to review the latest updates on these various plans. These plans are best if (1) parents don't expect to qualify for financial aid, (2) parents are conservative or novice investors, and (3) parents understand the risks.

HELOC or Second Mortgage

One of the reasons I refer you to chapter 5, "The 60-Minute Debt Workout," in regard to this particular topic is that it is a debt that stands in the way of your being able to become a conscientious investor. A HELOC (home equity line of credit) is not a good debt at all, because it deteriorates one of your highest-dollar-value assets: your home. So go to my tools at www.elliekay.com to crunch the numbers on what your HELOC or your second mortgage is costing you in terms of interest, and you'll find that one of the best investments you can make is to pay it off as soon as you can. Pay it off before you begin other kinds of investing.

Roth IRA and Traditional IRA

An individual retirement account (IRA) is a personal savings plan that allows you and your spouse to contribute up to $5,000 a year apiece. If you're fifty or older, you can make an additional $1,000 catch-up contribution. Every dollar you invest today will work for you until you stop working and are ready to start playing in retirement. The sooner you open an IRA, the more money you'll have for your golden years. I plan on doing a lot more skydiving and rock climbing, because I just don't seem to be able to schedule those on my calendar very often.

If you have earned income and are less than seventy and a half years old, then you may make a contribution to a traditional IRA. The only question is whether that contribution will be deductible. If it's not deductible, there are still benefits to funding your IRA annually, but that is a detail you can research in your sixty-minute workout. Whether your IRA is deductible or not depends on your income-tax filing status and whether you or your spouse participated on any day of the year in an employer's qualified retirement plan.

In general, if neither you nor your spouse participated in a 401(k) or other qualified retirement plan, your contribution will be fully deductible.

Roth IRA versus Traditional IRA

There are two basic IRA options that you should evaluate in order to continue to grow wealth through investments: a traditional IRA and a Roth IRA. Choose a Roth IRA if you can do without the tax break right now (or if you don't qualify for a tax-deductible IRA). It's a more flexible instrument, because

1. it allows you to withdraw your contributions at any time, penalty- and tax-free;
2. you do not have to take mandatory distributions at age seventy and a half.

Choose a traditional IRA if you need the tax deduction now, if you have not contributed to a 401(k) or SEP (simplified employee pension plan), or if you anticipate paying taxes at a significantly lower rate in retirement.

I fund our IRAs once a year. Everyone has until April 15 every year to make a contribution to an IRA for the previous year—it's not like you have to make it by December 31. This is good because it gives you time to gather the money to put into your IRA. I recommend that you figure out how much you'll contribute for the year (let's say $2,000 for you and $2,000 for your spouse), divide it by fifty-two weeks ($38.46 per person), and allocate that amount as an automatic withdrawal to go to the account you've set aside for funding your IRA. When it's automatic and made before you get your check, it's a lot easier to prioritize your expenditures. Your goal should be to work toward fully funding IRAs for both you and your spouse (a weekly allotment of $76.92). When tax day rolls around, you'll have funded your IRA and started saving for next year's contribution.

Investing

If you've completed all these other areas of saving and retirement, then it's time to look at other forms of investments, including mutual funds, exchange traded funds, bonds, and life in the world of the stock market. As I said earlier, these areas overlap because your 401(k) and IRA are invested in these as well. Keep in mind, though, that this book is not an investment book; it's a money workout book, and it's difficult to cover an investment topic in the space allotted here. It would take at least another fifty pages, and even then I would have only begun to cover the basics. I recommend that you purchase a couple of key books: Joel Greenblatt, *The Little Book That Beats the Market* (2006); Andrew Tobias, *The Only Investment Guide You'll Ever Need* (2005); and Burton G. Malkiel and Charles D. Ellis, *The Elements of Investing* (2009).

Whether you are a new investor or a longtime veteran, it's important to look at the five most common mistakes to avoid in order to find investing success.

1. **Impudence.** One of my pet peeves as a financial expert is when people don't take good advice, go their own way, fail miserably, and then complain about their bad situation as if they bear no responsibility whatsoever for their key mistakes. In some cases, these people try to blame others or circumstance or even God. But there's a fine line between prevention and presumption. In fact, there is an entire new field of study created by behavioral psychologists and financial economists to look at why people manage their money (and the blame) in the way they do. It's called behavioral finance. Make a successful investment or two and the average bear's (pardon the pun) stock soars and this investor believes he is a stock market genius. People confuse blind luck with skill. To avoid becoming overconfident and thereby making poor choices, think about the

tortoise and the hare. The slow, steady progress of a buy-and-hold investor (one who buys a diversified portfolio and then keeps it until retirement) is more likely to reach the finish line with a steady 9.6 percent growth than the investor who incurs unnecessary risks motivated by thinking a bit too much of his own investment ability.

2. **Buying high, selling low.** No investor in her right mind would buy an Internet stock at an all-time high price and then sell it two months later at an all-time low, right? Well, that's what investors did in late 1999 and early 2000 when they bought up high-tech and Internet stocks or invested in equity mutual funds that were heavily invested in these stocks. They lost their shirts because they thought they could time the market. They second-guessed the market, thinking that it still had a ways to go higher and they could still get in on the rise. Once again, buy-and-hold investors would not be a party to timing the market. Instead, they avoid riskier funds, avoid the timing penalty, and opt for value funds, which tend to hold their value over the course of market fluctuations and which eventually even out. That's why the 9.6 percent average return is a bit skewed, even for the buy-and-hold crowd. But even that crowd may come in at the top (the high value) and then out at the bottom (the low value), which would make that average return two points lower. So don't try to time the market.

3. **Groupthink.** Before I received my degree from Colorado Christian University in the management of human resources, we studied a number of behavioral responses evident in business. One that fascinated me was groupthink: a type of thought exhibited by members of a group who try to minimize conflict and reach consensus without critically testing, analyzing, or evaluating ideas. As we practiced this in an exercise in class, I learned a humiliating lesson. Basically, I led the groupthink effort to win a game against the other team at the expense and embarrassment of one of their team players. Not usually one to exercise such poor

judgment, I saw how following the crowd could have devastating effects. I never made that mistake again! In the marketplace, when you follow the herd, you'll end up panicking like so many did in the 2007 to 2009 bear market. They sold when their portfolios were low, just because everyone else did. The same can happen when the entire "in crowd" is buying at the high market tide. Be patient and you'll come out ahead over the long haul.

4. **Trying to predict the market.** One of our sons requested *The Best of the Tonight Show with Johnny Carson* DVD for his birthday recently, and we bought it for him. One of our favorite sketches is when Carson played Carnac the Magnificent, a psychic who wore a large, elaborate turban. He had a plethora of envelopes, all of which (according to his sidekick Ed McMahon) "a child of four could plainly see" were "hermetically sealed" and kept in "a mayonnaise jar on Funk and Wagnalls's porch since noon" that day. Carnac would announce an answer to the question sealed in each envelope and then open the envelope and read the question. It was comedy at its best. But those who try on the role of Carnac when it comes to the stock market demonstrate investing at its worst. In the field of behavioral finance, psychologists have identified a tendency in people to think they are in control when they are not. When investors try to spot a market trend in a stock chart and predict the future, they have a terminal case of Carnac the Magnificent, and it's not funny. Do not overvalue a losing stock in your portfolio because you think you "know something." Don't try to predict how a stock will perform based on its past performance. You just don't know, and you need to quit trying to be a psychic.

5. **Falling for fees.** When it comes to investing, you get to keep anything you don't have to pay out in fees! Beware of the costs of investing in certain mutual funds. Every one of them has a cost associated with it. Be very careful that your fund's growth is not cut in half by a high-expense fund manager.

Once you avoid the above mistakes and do your research, then you are ready to set up different kinds of investments, including IRAs, which are easy to do, to begin to invest on your own. Just follow these steps.

Step 1: Find a Discount Broker

If you don't already have one, I suggest that you look into opening a discount brokerage account. For example, Wells Fargo has an investment program with no stock trading fees for the first hundred trades per year—if you do your own investing online and if you have $25,000 in assets in their bank (which can be a mix of all types of accounts). For a complete chart that compares different brokerage firms and the fees associated with them, go to www.bankrate.com or get the latest issue of *Money* magazine (see their investors guide at www.cnnmoney.com) or *Kiplinger's Personal Finance* (www.kiplinger.com). Your broker should be able to handle IRAs, Roth IRAs, rollover accounts, spouse IRAs, and education IRAs.

Step 2: Open and Fund Your Account

Once you've compared discount brokers and decided which is the best fit for your financial needs, it is time to open your account. Most brokers have an application you can complete and submit online and allow you to electronically transfer funds from your checking or savings account. However, some brokers require that you print out the form and mail it to them with a check.

Step 3: Invest It!

Once your check or electronic transfer has cleared, you're ready to start investing. That means you need to decide which stocks or mutual funds you want to buy. If you are investing yourself (without the advice of a broker), then it is critical that you subscribe to the magazines listed in step 1 in order to find the best-performing stocks and bonds. Or if that's too much of a time commitment, then consult your broker for an opinion and instruct him to buy the stocks or mutual funds, thereby funding the account.

✓ The 60-Minute Retirement and Savings Plan Workout Tip Sheet

Now that you've done your pretest and reviewed the different savings and investing topics, you are ready to begin the workout. Gather the appropriate materials (computer, automatic allotment forms, IRA setup information, magazines, etc.) so you will have them at the ready.

1. Make-Up-Your-Mind Warmup (5 minutes)
- Say something positive about the results of the pretest to yourself and/or your spouse.
- Make a commitment to have a successful workout.

2. Strength Training (10 minutes)
- Write down the results of the pretest and use that to decide the topic of this workout: savings accounts, 401(k)s, college funding, IRAs, or other investing.
- List a means for overcoming the obstacles that have previously prevented you from succeeding in this area.

3. Cardio Burn (20 minutes)
- Reread the notes on your chosen topic and discuss all options with your mate if you are working out in tandem.
- Determine the steps you need to take today to implement your plan and which steps you can do during the time frame allotted in the next section.

4. Take Your Heart Rate (20 minutes)

- Go to the investment tool section of www.elliekay.com and access your topic of choice. Work through that tool calculator to get the information you need.
- Take proactive steps to implement the plan you discussed in the previous step (that is, get an automatic pay allotment form to start saving from your paycheck, get the information from magazines or online to accomplish your goals).

5. Congratulations Cool Down (5 minutes)

- Say something positive about your progress today and/or your spouse.
- Set the topic for your next workout.

The 60-Minute Debt Workout

I was honored to have the opportunity to appear on ABC's *Nightline* to do a show about helping a family get out of excessive credit card debt. The publicists, the *Nightline* producers, and my own office set out to find a family who was willing to be filmed as I walked them through the process of what it takes to get out of debt and to negotiate with credit card lenders for lower interest rates. You would not believe the e-mails and contacts we received from across the country—we had hit a nerve with so many people desperate to get out of consumer debt. But finding the right couple who were willing to be put on camera in front of five million viewers was a completely different story. We finally found a woman whose husband was in the military and they lived in different cities. When I went to her home and crunched her numbers, she got the shock of a lifetime. She thought she had around $56,000 in consumer debt, but when we crunched the numbers, she actually had almost $109,000 in debt because of her home equity line of credit (HELOC). She had taken out this loan against her home to pay off other consumer debt, and she just spent it. Because it was an unsecured loan and/or used to pay off consumer debt, it was treated just like any other kind of consumer debt.

When I asked her how long it would take to pay off that debt ($60,000 in credit cards, not the HELOC) by only paying the minimums, she guessed twenty years. But this poor lady was in for another shock: at an interest rate of 18 percent (which was the rate on some of her cards), it would take eighty-seven years to pay off her debt. At an interest rate of 9 percent (what we were trying to get for her), it would take thirty-five years. Her face fell as hope left the room and the camera rolled. That is the cancerous result of debt. This woman was living the consequences of a life of excessive debt.

- Debt puts a marriage at risk.
- Debt makes you a servant to the lender.
- Debt borrows from your future and your children's future.
- Debt hinders sharing with others.
- Debt erodes resources through high interest payments.

But I didn't want to leave her hopeless, so I told her, "If you pay only 3 percent more than the minimum payment, and we can get your interest rates down to 9 percent, then you can be out of consumer debt in only three and a quarter years!"

I coached her on what to say to get her credit card interest rates reduced, and she was successful in getting those rates down to only 9 percent across the board!

You can find all the tools or calculators I used to determine minimum payments and early payoff on my Web site. These tools are very sophisticated and are the same ones found on such sites as www.bankrate.com and www.abcnews.go.com/business.

This hour will cultivate a systematic way to pay down debt using a variety of options, from the snowball effect to selling unused assets to cutting back on expenses.

Preworkout Test

You may not know if you really have a debt problem yet. You may have thought, *Hey, I've put on a few dollars here and there, but I can quit any time.* There's no more effective way to see if you have a problem than to step on the scale. Here are some indicators that you need to go on a debt diet. Read and check all the statements that apply to you.

- I use credit card cash advances to pay for living expenses.
- I use and depend on overtime to meet my monthly expenses.
- I have a steadily increasing revolving balance on my credit cards.
- I use credit to buy things that I used to pay cash for, such as groceries, gasoline, and clothing (and I do not pay off the full amount when the credit card bill arrives).
- I use the overdraft protection plan on my checking account to pay monthly bills.
- I use savings to pay bills.
- I use one credit card to pay another.
- I float my bills: delaying one bill in order to pay another over-due bill.
- I use another loan or an extension on a loan to service my debt.
- I use a cosigner on a note.
- I pay only the minimum amounts due on charge accounts.
- I have a FICO (Fair Isaac) score of less than 550. (This is the credit score that lenders often use to evaluate creditworthiness.)

Test Results

If two or more of these statements fit your situation, then you need to go on a debt diet. If five or more fit you, you are financially obese and will likely default on serious loans within the year. Now is the time to fight this good fight. Now is the time for the faith that you can do it. Now is the time for financial freedom.

The 60-Minute Debt Workout

This chapter is one of the most important chapters in this book, and if you have consumer debt, then this workout will be one that you will want to repeat often. For this workout, you will need to choose one of four different debt workouts. If you want to look at all of them before you decide, that is fine. Unlike other workouts, reading ahead will not spoil the spontaneity of your answers.

1. Make-Up-Your-Mind Warmup (5 minutes)

Remember that progress is success. So if you have an hour where you do nothing more than add up all your debt (for the liability chart), then that's a success! If you have another session where you work through and fill out the asset chart, then that, too, is success! Learn to embrace the positive in this process, and don't let your mind dwell on any despairing or disparaging thoughts or ideas. Stop all negative self-talk. Stop beating yourself up for your debt problems. You've done enough of that already. Start by saying something positive about the pretest such as, "At least I answered false to quite a few of those scenarios!"

Next, choose from one of the four following debt workouts:

- Liability Chart
- Snowball Debt Repayment Plan
- Asset Chart
- Money Move Debt Education Exercise

2. Strength Training (10 minutes)

List any obstacles (on the pretest and others you can think of) that are in your way of becoming free of consumer debt. Maybe some of these obstacles include medical bills, unemployment, or caring for elderly parents. A wide variety of things may have contributed to your situation. The important thing is for you to evaluate your debt on a personal level and to do this with your spouse if you are working in tandem.

List the means of overcoming every obstacle on your list, even if you just write "will work out on this again" to find a resolution or means of overcoming the obstacle. Place this list in the pocket folder you have marked "The 60-Minute Debt Workout."

3. Cardio Burn (20 minutes)

Read the detailed notes on your chosen workout (listed in the previous warmup). This will take a bit of time as you read for understanding. If you are working out with a partner, please make sure he is up to speed, and respect the boundaries listed in chapter 1 as you work alongside him.

Go to my Web site and use the appropriate tool for your situation. Here is a list of those debt and credit tools:
- Accelerated Debt Payoff Calculator
- Debt Calculator
- Debt Payoff Goal Calculator
- ARM APR Calculator
- Credit Card Minimum Payment Interest Calculator
- Debt Ratio Calculator
- Bi-Weekly or Monthly Loan Calculator
- Bi-Weekly vs. Monthly Loan Calculator
- Interest-Only Loan Payment Calculator
- Interest Only vs. Principal and Interest Payment Calculator
- Auto Loan vs. Home Equity Loan Calculator
- Automobile Loan Payment Calculator
- Fixed vs. Minimum Payment Calculator
- Loan Payment Calculator with Amortization Schedule
- Simple Loan Calculator
- Rent vs. Buy Calculator
- Credit Card Minimum Payment Interest Calculator
- Credit Card Fixed vs. Minimum Payment Calculator
- Loan Payment Calculator with Amortization Schedule

Crunch the numbers using these tools and print out copies for your pocket folder "The 60-Minute Debt Workout."

4. Take Your Heart Rate (20 minutes)

This is a section where some hard work begins. Fill in the charts with details for liabilities and/or assets, depending upon the debt workout you have chosen for the day. If you chose the snowball debt reduction plan, then put it down on paper, and use the above tools to work out any kinks. If taking the education test, work through the questions and answers.

5. Congratulations Cool Down (5 minutes)

The first time you do this workout, it might be very challenging or very exhilarating, you never can tell. But just like any other physical workout at the gym, it's not a stand-alone workout. For it to be effective, you have to repeat it with regularity. So conclude this session by saying something positive about your progress today and also something positive to your spouse if you worked out together. Set the time and topic for your next workout.

Debt Workout No. 1: The Liability Chart

What Are Your Current Liabilities?

Just as in the *Nightline* example I used at the beginning of this chapter, our subject didn't know how much consumer debt she had. Most people don't know exactly how much they owe. The liabilities you list on the following chart gives you an accurate picture of your current financial position. This step also helps determine what you need to pay off before you can begin to build savings and investments. The ideal situation is to be free of consumer debt and only carry mortgage and/or transportation debt before you start to invest. This will free you to establish a debt repayment schedule for each creditor and to decide which debts to pay off first.

Now is also a good time to order a free copy of your credit report and check it against your records. You may think you owe $350 to JCPenney, but the credit report may indicate you really owe $750. This can impact you and your spouse's FICO score, which determines everything from what premium you pay on your insurance bill to the interest rate on your mortgage to whether that future employer will hire you or your spouse!

Due to federal consumer protection laws, everyone is allowed to receive a free copy of his or her credit report every year from each of the three credit bureaus. This means you can get a free copy every four months. Write down the following agencies in your smartphone or calendar to remind you to order one of the three free credit report copies every four months. Yours is separate from your spouse's. This tiny tip can save you big bucks and/or a major migraine when it comes to identity theft or other credit-related headaches.

You may order each of your free copies from:

www.annualcreditreport.com

Annual Credit Report Request Service

PO Box 105281

Atlanta, GA 30348-5281

For further reference:

- Equifax, www.equifax.com, 1-800-685-1111
- Experian, www.experian.com, 1-888-397-3742
- TransUnion, www.transunion.com, 1-800-888-4213

Debt Workout No. 2: Paying Off Debt with the Snowball Plan

I know you've heard some financial experts say that paying off the credit card or loan with the highest interest rate first is the way to go. These experts have math on their side. But I suppose I'm a little different, because I remember a quote from Chuck Swindoll that has stuck with me for more than a decade: "The longer I live the more convinced I become that life is 10 percent what happens to us and 90 percent how we respond to it."[1] I think this is especially true in finances. Having fewer bills to pay and paying off more bills gets you motivated and keeps you going when the debt reduction gets hard. It's important to knock out some of those smaller debts, even if they have a lower interest rate, just so you'll see significant progress.

You can count how many cards or debts you've paid off and see fewer

Liability Chart

Liability/Loan	Total Balance Due	Minimum Payment	Months Until Payoff
Home			
HELOC			
Car #1			
Car #2			
Furniture			
Student Loans			
Boat/RV/Luxury Items			
Outstanding Taxes/IRS			
Department Store Cards (list separately)			
_____			
_____			
Credit Cards (list separately)			
_____			
_____			
Totals			

and fewer left on your liability chart. Now that's what I call motivating. It worked for Bob and me, and it can work for you as well. It's called the snowball effect for a reason.

When we were stationed in Fort Drum, New York, we got 120 inches of snow the first January we were there! One month alone! Our kids weren't used to the fluffy white stuff. They were ages two, four, six, eight, and ten the first time it came down. I bundled them up in snowsuits, and we had a ball—a snowball that is. It started small, but as we rolled it across the front lawn, it became bigger and bigger! Pretty soon it was so big that we couldn't roll it anymore.

When Bob came home, he helped us roll it toward the big sledding hill in our backyard, and it went up and over. It took a village of Kays to make it happen! As it gained momentum going down the hill, it also gained in size *and* speed. It was great fun to see it come to its resting place at the base of the hill. We followed in plastic sleds.

The debt principle is the same in that you will put all your resources toward one debt while making minimum payments on other debts in order to focus on one line of credit at a time. Otherwise, it can seem frustrating, because your efforts don't seem to add up to much. You don't want to pay down debt by wiping out your savings account to do it, as that can lead to more debt if you don't have at least $1,000 cash as an emergency fund. Begin to concentrate your efforts on one debt at a time, with the goal of getting rid of everything except for mortgage debt. Using the liability chart from your previous debt workout, list debts in order, with the smallest payoff or balance first. Remember we're not concentrating on interest rates at this point. If you have two debts that have similar balances, then list the higher interest rate debt first.

Keep the paid-off bills in your pocket file folder from "The 60-Minute Debt Workout" or post them in your utility room as a visual reminder of what you've paid off. The snowball effect intensifies with each debt you pay off, and then you can increase the next monthly debt payment by using the extra money you used to pay off the first debt. As you pay off the smaller balances and begin to tackle the larger debts, you also have more money to tackle them with because you've been eliminating payments as you go.

Be sure to pay the minimum payments on the other debts so you don't deteriorate your FICO score in your effort to get yet another bill paid down. You will find that paying off the little debts first gives you quick results, and you are more likely to stay motivated to continue to push that debt snowball plan until it's out of your yard completely. Don't stop at consumer debt and revolving loans, go ahead and pay off the cars (see how to drive cars for free in chapter 4, "The 60-Minute Retirement and Savings Workout"). Take it from someone who knows, debt makes life ugly, but financial freedom is *beautiful*!

The Asset Chart

What Are Your Current Assets?

By filling in your liability chart, you've already faced your first time of reckoning. Now, as you complete the asset chart, you will subtract your liabilities from your assets to establish your net worth. For some people, their net worth is a negative number, but you're in famous company, because Donald Trump was once worth negative millions. That's why I want to help you get rid of debt and increase your net worth. Once this chart is completed, you'll also have an idea of what you might be able to sell to pay down your debt. In some cases, people are so motivated to live a debt-free life that they decide to move to a less expensive home or sell a car to pay cash for an older vehicle, which is something I addressed in chapter 4, "The 60-Minute Retirement and Savings Workout." As you fill out this chart, you will need to do your due diligence and follow through on the appropriate research to get an accurate number. For example, you may have more equity in your home than you think. Call your mortgage company and see what numbers they have or go to www.zillow.com to crunch your own numbers with a very rough idea of the fair market value of your

home. Do the same for car loans. Go to www.edmunds.com or www.kbb
.com to determine the private-party value of your vehicles. You might find
that the car you think is an asset has little or no actual cash value due to
the amount-owed ratio versus the private-party value. Or you might find
that a car you thought was worth $12,000 would actually bring $14,500.

For other assets—such as antiques, electronics, or even childhood baseball cards—go to www.ebay.com, www.google.com, www.fatwallet.com,
or www.mysimon.com to get fair market values.

The final part of this step is going to be a time of self-reflection. Are
you willing to part with this asset to meet your goal of becoming debt
free? You may not be required to do so once all the numbers are crunched,
but the gut-level question is this: Would you be willing to part with this
material asset to venture into financial freedom? We did and we did not
regret it, because it was just one step on the way to building lasting wealth.

Two words of caution when it comes to asset liquidation to accommodate your debt diet:

1.   Always consider the tax ramifications before selling any assets.
2.   Never sacrifice long-term assets for short-term living expenses.

In other words, if part of your personal plan is to open a home equity
line of credit to pay down credit card debt, then you need to change that
plan! Or if you think, *I can always cash in my 401(k),* then think again! It
would be far better to move to another home with a lower monthly payment than to cannibalize equity in order to pay down debt. Simplify your
assets and maximize your debt reduction and savings accounts.

Money Move Debt Education Exercise

This section is different from the previous ones in this chapter because its
primary purpose is to gain some additional knowledge about key money
moves. Your answers to these questions may be keeping you in debt, and
it's important to understand what money moves you should make and
which ones you should avoid.

Asset Chart

Asset Name	Amount Owed (If Applicable)	Equity or Actual Cash Value (ACV)	Can Sell or Liquidate? (Yes or No)
Home	N/A	_____	_____
Other Real Estate	N/A	_____	_____
Savings	N/A	_____	_____
Checking	N/A	_____	_____
Mutual Funds	N/A	_____	_____
Money Market	N/A	_____	_____
Stocks/Bonds	N/A	_____	_____
Retirement Plan	N/A	_____	_____
Other Funds	N/A	_____	_____
Cars	_____	_____	_____
Furniture	_____	_____	_____
Jewelry	_____	_____	_____
Household Goods	_____	_____	_____
Boat/RV/Luxury Items	_____	_____	_____
Antiques/Other	_____	_____	_____

Top Ten "Money Moves" Quiz

Consider the following ten statements in light of your attitudes or actions. Rate each with either Agree, Maybe, or Disagree. Save your results for after the quiz.

1. I have a large mortgage because all mortgage debt is good debt.
2. I'll just use a home equity loan to pay off credit card debt.
3. I'll put it on my credit card.
4. I need to drive a really nice or new car, because it will save on maintenance and I'll have a warranty.
5. We always get a big tax refund.
6. I'm going to borrow from my 401(k)/IRA. I'll look into the details later.
7. I'm not building my 401(k) in this kind of market.
8. I invest in this company because I know it.
9. I don't want to contribute to a nondeductible IRA because there's no immediate tax benefit.
10. I should probably refinance, but it really seems like a hassle.

Answers: Top Ten "Money Moves" Quiz

1. "I have a large mortgage because all mortgage debt is good debt." **Disagree.**

    The recent mortgage meltdown where people bought more house than their debt-to-income ratios would allow is reason enough to avoid getting overmortgaged in a house you cannot afford. One major reason for debt gain has to do with the good news/bad news of recent mortgage rates. The bad news is that too many people lost their homes to foreclosures. The good news is that the fat practices of mortgage brokers are a thing of the recent and harmful past. It's harder to get a home loan today. You have to put more money down, and you'll have to prove you have the ability to pay based on debt-to-income ratios.

When it comes to mortgages, the good debt/bad debt logic has officially broken down.

The mortgages that many homeowners had were much larger than they might have been in the past due to lower interest rates and the availability of adjustable rate mortgages (ARMs). Furthermore, many homeowners took advantage of rising home values and used some of the equity in their homes to pay off consumer debt through home equity lines of credit (HELOC). But even though HELOC rates were lower than some credit card rates, they were also higher than regular mortgage rates, and they were destructive in that they diminished the equity in the homes. When ARMs adjusted and home values plummeted, these homeowners were upside down in their homes, owing more than they could pay, and they lost their greatest asset.

2. "I'll just use a home equity loan to pay off credit card debt."
   Disagree.

   I alluded to this above, but why is this specifically a dumb money move? Lenders love to tout the benefits of robbing Peter to pay Paul. When home equity rates are down, it seems like a good move, right? Wrong. According to the Federal Reserve, in 2009 we borrowed $701.5 billion from our home equities, which is up $416.2 billion from the previous decade. The only way this truly helps is if you completely stop using credit cards to run up those debts and then pay off the HELOC—an act of discipline that the average American simply will not do. Therefore, unless you're well above average, using debt to pay off debt is *never* a good move. Your debt hole only gets deeper, and you don't even realize it because you're still making your mortgage payment and not looking at the bottom line of your total debt load.

   In recent years, nearly two-thirds of the people who borrowed against the equity in their homes to pay off credit cards instead have run up more credit card debt, according to a study by Atlanta research firm Britain Associates.[2] This move slowly whittles away the equity you have in your home for use in case of an emergency, such as unemployment, medical expenses, or other financial setbacks.

3. "I'll put it on my credit card." **Disagree.**

If your credit card works out more than you do, you likely have a debt problem. For example, some consumers feel that by using their credit cards for daily purchases they're building airline miles or they have an interest-free loan until the bill comes due. But buying on credit makes it far easier to overspend. Paying cash is a more conscientious decision, no matter how you look at it. The average person is less likely to buy whenever the urge hits if he or she is constantly forking over twenty-dollar bills to pay for purchases. Plus fees on credit cards are becoming more and more prevalent and more costly.

There are two kinds of debt: good debt and bad debt. A mortgage is an example of good debt, but consumer debt is bad debt. Your credit card debt may either be in the card or in your mortgage (on a home equity loan), but the debt is still there, waiting to be erased.

According to www.cardweb.com, the average family's debt load in 2009 was $8,940. That's expensive weight to carry around, making the family more at risk for an average 16 percent APR for most cards. The amazing fact is that the average family has not only one card but sixteen! That typically includes six bank cards, eight retail cards, and two or three debit cards among the family members.

4. "I need to drive a really nice or new car, because it will save on maintenance and I'll have a warranty." **Disagree.**

Americans are in love with their cars. Our fantasy includes a big house, nice cars, and dream vacations. While we might get good interest rates on our home and economize on vacations, it's usually the car craze that loads us down with debt. According to the Consumer Bankers Association,[3] the average new vehicle loan has increased 5 percent to $24,779, and the average used vehicle loan rose 12 percent to $18,542. The trend toward longer loans means that the average consumer will have a car that will not be paid for in less than forty-nine months. By the time you trade in the car for a new one, the old car is often worth less than the remaining loan value. Buying a new car every five years, as most Americans do, while still owing on the old one, continues to add debt upon debt.

Is it only car and mortgage debt that is weighing us down? Unfortunately, no. We have smart people making dumb money moves that keep them from paying off debt even when they have the means to do so.

5. "We always get a big tax refund." **Disagree.**

The operative word here is *big*, meaning more than around $2,900 or so, which was the average tax refund for 2009,[4] with 75 percent of taxpayers getting a refund. If you are getting this much back in a refund, then you are likely overwithholding on your taxes. Some people just like getting that check every year so they can spend it on vacations, luxury items, or paying off an item they bought in anticipation of the refund. Most tax professionals are exasperated with clients who are getting upward of $10,000 in refunds and act happy about it. It's usually best to adjust your W-4 to have less withheld rather than having the forced savings of a refund. That way, your money earns interest for *you* through-out the year, instead of sitting stagnant, waiting for you to get it back in the form of a tax refund.

It's wiser to adjust the W-4 to the correct number of deduc-tions, and then use that available income to create a direct deposit into a savings plan or use it to pay off consumer debt. You really can trust yourself to save more and let your money make money for you throughout the year—not just at tax time.

6. "I'm going to borrow from my 401(k)/IRA. I'll look into the details later." **Disagree.**

    The younger your family, the more likely you are to make a dumb money move without knowing the details (penalties, restrictions, and limitations involved) of a financial decision like this. Let's say you take $50,000 in early distributions (withdrawals, not loans) from a 401(k) and IRA to buy a home because you thought you could do so without penalty.

    I'm amazed at how many long-term decisions are made as a result of getting casual (and bad) information over a water-cooler conversation! It's important to check with your tax software program (such as www.taxact.com) before you make a major financial decision. Or go to www.irs.gov and sign up for regular e-mail alerts so that you can get information year-round.

7. "I'm not building my 401(k) in this kind of market." **Disagree.**

    Don't deprive yourself of a tax-deferred savings plan for the future because the market is down today. Furthermore, you shouldn't deprive yourself of free money if your employer is matching your contributions! Even if your employer's match is down or if the market is down, you don't have to invest your 401(k) in stocks. You can put your money in a low-risk bond or a money market fund until the market bounces back.

8. "I invest in this company because I know it." **Disagree.**

    Suppose a doctor is fond of investing in a particular pharmaceutical company because he is familiar with their products and services. Is that a good reason to buy their stock? No. Similarly, employees tend to own too much of their employer's company stock because they're overconfident about knowing when to sell. They feel they'll see the writing on the wall internally. I'll sum up that faulty logic in one word: Enron.

The best advice is to never invest more than 10 percent of your portfolio in any one stock and never more than 30 percent in a particular sector—even if the company is owned by your mother!

9. "I don't want to contribute to a nondeductible IRA because there's no immediate tax benefit." **Disagree.**

You would end up not investing in any kind of IRA at all, and the future will not fund itself. The money you put into an IRA might not be tax-deductible, but the interest that grows from that fund is still tax-deferred. This means the money can grow faster than it might in a taxable account, where you'll pay taxes every year on dividends, capital gains, and interest to Uncle Sam and to your home state.

10. "I should probably refinance, but it really seems like a hassle." **Disagree.**

The only reason you should not refinance isn't because of the hassle, but because of the bottom line. If you crunch the numbers at my tool section at www.elliekay.com for the amount of time it takes to shop for a loan, fill out the paperwork, and project the overall benefit, then you'll find it truly could be worth the "hassle." For example, if you can save $3,600 per year with a refinanced mortgage, and the process takes about ten hours, then you are making around $360 an hour! This is guaranteed income (and tax free, I might add) and usually worth the time. Just make sure the numbers add up to your advantage in order to make this a smart money move for you.

Assessing Your Debt Knowledge

Give yourself one point for each question you answered Agree, two points for each Maybe, and three points for each Disagree.

Financially Fit. If you scored between 26 and 30, then you weren't swayed by any of the gimmicks or tricks found in the suggested money moves and you are financially fit (not to mention smart).

Mild Problem. If you scored between 22 and 26, then you have a mild debt problem and may want to lose a few pounds to be at top form.

Moderate Problem. If your score was between 18 and 22, then you are susceptible to making some dumb money moves that could keep you in debt for most of your life. You most likely live above your means and have a mounting debt problem. It would be wise to develop a better understanding of debt and begin a path toward the right attitudes and actions that will help you improve your financial status.

Mongo Problem. If you scored less than 18, then you clearly have a significant debt problem that will weigh you down and keep you from reaching the finish line of your financial goals. You need to take deliberate, disciplined action to overcome the problem. If you continue down the path you are currently on, you will likely end up in need of the financial equivalent of gastric bypass; namely, bankruptcy and/or no retirement funds or no financial legacy to pass on to your children. But even in your case, there is still hope for your future.

✓ The 60-Minute Debt Workout Tip Sheet

1. Make-Up-Your-Mind Warmup (5 minutes)
- Say something positive about the results of the pretest or otherwise.
- Commit to establishing the debt topic you will follow for this workout (Liability Chart, Snowball Debt Payment Plan, Asset Chart, Money Move Debt Education Exercise).
- Commit to finding success in this workout.

2. Strength Training (10 minutes)
- Write down the results of the pretest.
- List the obstacles (on the pretest and others you can think of) that have gotten in the way of your becoming free of consumer debt.
- List the means of overcoming these obstacles.

3. Cardio Burn (20 minutes)
- Reread the detailed notes on your chosen workout (listed in the warmup above).
- Go to www.elliekay.com and use the appropriate tool that fits your situation (see the list in detailed workout section).
- Crunch the numbers using the tools from www.elliekay.com and print out copies for your pocket folder "The 60-Minute Debt Workout."

4. Take Your Heart Rate (20 minutes)
- Fill in the charts with details about your liability and assets.
- Work through a snowball debt reduction plan on paper and by using the tools found at www.elliekay.com.
- If you are taking the education test, work through the questions and answers.

5. Congratulations Cool Down (5 minutes)
- Say something positive about your progress today to yourself and/or your spouse.
- Set the time and topic for your next workout.

The 60-Minute Cha Ching Guide to Paying Less Workout

Bob, our son Jonathan, and I were in the home office working feverishly on our individual projects. Bob was concentrating on his article for *Checkpoints,* the U.S. Air Force Academy alumni magazine. Jonathan was writing an essay for his English class. And I was working on an Operation Homefront column. Suddenly, we heard some loud thuds, grunts, and banging noises from Joshua's room. The youngest of four boys and three girls, Joshua's often been labeled the most aggressive, but this was loud even for him.

Jonathan said what all of us were thinking: "What in the world is he doing in there?"

I looked around and couldn't see our puppies, Buddy and Anna, so I suggested, "Maybe he's wrestling with the dogs."

A few minutes later, Joshua flounced into the office, plopped in a chair, and loudly gulped for air. He was heaving and gasping as if he were desperately out of breath. It was pretty obvious he was waiting for us to ask "the" question.

"What on earth have you been doing, Joshua?" Bob obliged. "Why are you so out of breath?"

With a straight face and a most nonchalant attempt at trying to sound utterly cool, he replied, "Oh, me? I've just been practicing some dance moves that my friend taught me." He shook his bangs in a Zac Efron head toss.

Jonathan and I locked gazes, then I looked at Joshua again, who was completely serious. The corner of Jonathan's mouth started to curl up, and I realized he was thinking of the same lines from the movie *Napoleon Dynamite* as I was:

LaFawnduh: "Why are you so sweaty?"

Napoleon Dynamite: "I've been practicing."

LaFawnduh: "Mmm. Practicing what?"

Napoleon Dynamite: "Some dance moves."

We were both trying not to laugh, and we succeeded until Joshua left the room to go back to his dance moves. Then we burst out laughing.

Who needs to spend money on dance lessons when you can get tips from a friend? Who needs to spend money on entertainment when you have the youngest child of seven to entertain you? There are lots of conventional (and unconventional) ways to save money if you put forth the effort and know how to do the right moves in your dance to cut costs in a variety of ways.

Whether you *want* to save or you *have* to save, here are the best tips I've gleaned from my experience. While they are not exhaustive, they will get you started. For more ways to save, refer to my book *The Little Book of Big Savings* (WaterBrook, 2009) for under $10.

Preworkout Shopping Quiz

Food

How much do you currently pay for food per month per adult?

(a) Less than $171

(b) Between $172 and $217

(c) Between $218 and $267

(d) More than $267

How many homemade family-dinner meals do you make each week?
(a) 6 to 7
(b) 4 to 5
(c) 2 to 3
(d) 0 to 1

How many prepared (frozen, ready-to-eat) family-dinner meals do you make each week?
(a) 0 to 1
(b) 2 to 3
(c) 4 to 5
(d) 6 to 7

How often do you take advantage of price rollbacks?
(a) Every time I shop
(b) Frequently
(c) Occasionally
(d) What's a price rollback? (That is, never.)

How often do you take advantage of price guarantees (the store honors advertisements from competitors' sale ads)?
(a) Almost every time I shop
(b) Frequently
(c) Occasionally
(d) Never

Entertainment

How many meals do you and family members eat out each week? (Count each meal eaten out separately. For example, a family of four eating dinner would count as four meals.)
(a) 0 to 2
(b) 3 to 4

(c) 5 to 6
(d) 7 or more

How many full-price movie tickets do you purchase each week? (Matinee or discounted tickets count as half a ticket)
(a) 0 to 2
(b) 3 to 4
(c) 5 to 6
(d) 7 or more

How many new-release movies do you rent each week? (Non–new releases count as half, and a monthly movie pass counts as three per week).
(a) 0 to 2
(b) 3 to 4
(c) 5 to 6
(d) 7 or more

How many "treat dates" do you fund for your friends or family each week? (A treat is counted as one per ice cream, coffee drink, smoothie, milk shake, etc. A family of four going out for Frappuccinos would count as four treats.)
(a) 0 to 3
(b) 4 to 6
(c) 7 to 9
(d) 10 or more

How often do you or your family participate in other special event excursions and/or services per week? (Count as one per paid admission to a zoo, amusement park, skating, bowling, paintballing, spa treatments, manicures, pedicures, facials, etc.)
(a) 0 to 1
(b) 2 to 3

(c) 4 to 5
(d) 6 or more

Transportation
How many individual trips do you make to the grocery store, department store, discount store, electronics store, the mall, or other shopping venues each week? (Count each individual trip as one, and count combined trips as one.)
(a) 0 to 3
(b) 4 to 6
(c) 7 to 9
(d) 10 or more

If the speed limit is 65 mph, how fast do you normally drive?
(a) 60 mph to 65 mph; I'm a cautious driver.
(b) 66 mph to 70 mph; I push it just a little.
(c) 71 mph to 75 mph; I like to keep up with traffic.
(d) 75 mph or more: I live in the fast lane, baby!

How often do you have the air pressure checked in your tires?
(a) At least every other week
(b) Once a month or once every two months
(c) Once every three to six months
(d) Am I supposed to check the air?

How often, per week, do you carpool to work, to the kids' school, or to other events with friends (meetings, out-of-town trips, shopping)?
(a) 5 or more; I regularly carpool.
(b) 3 to 4; I try to make the driving count.
(c) 1 to 2; I'm a taxi mom.
(d) Never; I like to drive!

How often do you shop around for the best price on gas before you fill up?

(a) Every time; gas is too expensive to pay top price!

(b) Frequently; I pay attention to who has the best prices.

(c) Occasionally; when I can remember.

(d) Never; who has the time?

Quiz Results

Assign the points below for each letter in the above quiz. Then add up the total number for each letter as follows in each category. You will have different scores for food, entertainment, and transportation and will be able to see where you rank in each section:

a = 4 points

b = 3 points

c = 2 points

d = 1 point

16–20 points, Thrifty Tayna: Well done, you're a supersmart shopper! When it comes to shopping, preparing, and serving food in your home, you get the prize for being the smartest shopper on the block. You shop the sales, know how to get the best values, and make your family proud. You are well prepared for financial issues that arise in today's economy and can be in a position to help others learn to be smarter shoppers as well. When it comes to entertainment, you go to matinees, find coupons for special events, and get buy-one-get-one-free specials. You also do your research when buying gas by going to Web sites, carpooling when possible, and getting free coffee or a fill up with each tank you buy.

11–15 points, Low-Cost Logan: Good job, you're a smart shopper. You are doing a good job at keeping costs down for food, entertainment, and gasoline, thereby making good use of your dollars. While there is slight room for improvement, you are in a nice position to continue to be smart with your dollars and even help your children learn to be smart shoppers, budget their entertainment dollars, and even learn to conserve gasoline.

6–10 points, Moderate Morgan: Nice work, you are a shopper. There are some areas where you're doing better than others, and there's always room for improvement. By shopping for price rollbacks, creating more foods from scratch, and learning about price comparisons, you can learn to save a lot and become a smart shopper. You could also consider looking for entertainment values and trying to carpool in order to save on gas.

5 points, Extravagant Eric: You are one who shops! There's a difference between just shopping to get what you need and shopping with an eye for savings. You also spend excessively on entertainment, paying full price even when there might be a special you could take advantage of. In some cases, the most extravagant spenders tend to be less conservative when it comes to economizing on natural resources—such as gasoline. Although you scored in the high-spending spectrum of the quiz, it only means that you have the most potential to learn to save! There are a lot of strategies that can help. Learn to steer away from a steady fare of frozen and convenience foods and make a few more homemade meals. If you buy food when there are significant savings such as sales and low-price guarantees, you'll do much better. Just think, you're beginning to learn to shop smart!

The 60-Minute Cha Ching Guide to Paying Less Workout

1. Make-Up-Your-Mind Warmup (5 minutes)

This is going to be a really fun workout for some of you. Start by taking a deep breath and then saying something positive about the results of the pretest. Look at your best categories and congratulate yourself on the areas you do quite well in saving money. Commit to taking your "paying less" skills to the next level to save some serious change.

One other area you will cover in the warmup is to decide what you will do with your specific savings. It's not enough to reduce costs if what you save is just spent somewhere else. It's as if you never saved any money at all. You can direct your savings to paying off consumer debt, building up a savings account, planning for a special vacation, saving to pay cash for a car, etc.

2. Strength Training (10 minutes)

Write down the results of the pretest, looking at the areas where you may need some improvement. Decide on a section in this chapter where you need to reduce costs, such as food, transportation, insurance, or gently used clothing. Entertainment and travel will be covered in the next workout, so if that is an area you need to work on, be sure to do "The 60-Minute Travel and Fun Guide Workout."

List the current obstacles to saving money in these areas and write down some means of overcoming these obstacles, as indicated on the pretest. Create a pocket folder for "The 60-Minute Cha Ching Guide to Paying Less" and put your notes in this folder for future reference.

3. Cardio Burn (20 minutes)

Read the detailed notes on this section if necessary. If your category isn't covered, then get the other resources suggested or go to my blog at www.elliekay.com to do further research for your area.

Determine what your previous spending in this area has been and make a note of the amounts, using past bank statements or bills. Compare prices and do some research.

4. Take Your Heart Rate (20 minutes)

Implement your cost-reduction plan and print out any documentation for your pocket folder.

Write down a step-by-step plan to save money in this category. If you are involving other family members, delegate responsibilities. Track your savings and keep records in the pocket folder for this workout. Implement how you will funnel your savings into other categories (debt reduction, savings account, etc). For example, if you are saving money in the grocery store, you may want to immediately write a check to your savings account at the checkout. Or once you save on your insurance, put that amount toward your debt reduction.

5. Congratulations Cool Down (5 minutes)

Say something positive about your progress today and/or about your spouse. Set a time and topic for your next workout. This kind of a workout is easy to repeat at another time, and each time you will be cutting costs. It's an excellent way to become debt free and build a savings account for special purposes.

Suggested Categories for Paying Less

Insurance

I was an insurance broker for several years before I met and married Bob. This is one area where a few minor changes can yield big savings. Here are some quick ways to reduce insurance premiums for your automobile and household goods:

USAA. This is a great insurance company for military families. Not only do they cover auto and homeowners insurance, they offer dividends back on policies at the end of the accounting year. The longer you are with the company, the greater your dividend check. We've received anywhere from $100 to almost $1,000, which are unexpected sources of income. Bob has been with them for thirty years now!

Homeowners. Carry only the coverage you need; do not overinsure. If your home is valued at $150,000, and you insure it with replacement value for $200,000 and it burns down, they will only pay $150,000, and you've overpaid the premium. Keep in mind that the insurance price of the home does not include the land. Get a copy of your homeowners policy and call your provider, telling them that you believe you are paying too much. Be sure that you cover some of the specifics listed below. If they do not give you the price you want, then shop around.

- **Homeowners deductibles.** Carry a $500, $1,000, or 1 percent deductible on your homeowners policy.
- **Home Improvement.** If you get a new roof or new security system or make any other improvements, be sure your insurance company knows about them. It could save you even more on your policy.
- **Special Riders.** Check with your insurance company to see its limitations on personal articles. Jewelry, collections, antiques, computers, and guns may all need to be added as riders to get full coverage on these personal items. Insurance companies will only cover a minimum on these without a rider.

Flood insurance. Remember that flood insurance is only sold by the state, and you are not covered unless you've purchased this policy from the government.

Tenant policies. If you do not own your home or you live in base housing, then you will need to get a tenant policy. Ask for a nonsmoker discount if you qualify, and shop around. You will want to get replacement value and special riders if necessary.

Automobile. Research your prices at www.progressive.com and then take those prices back to your existing provider to see if they can match the price. Be sure to compare apples with apples, meaning you have the same coverage, deductibles, etc.

Youthful drivers. You might have to put a car title in a teenage driver's name in order to be able to save even more. Check with your agent because the rules on this vary from state to state. Taking driver's education is another good way to get a ticket off your record or a discount on your policy.

Uninsured motorists. If you are driving a car that does not carry full coverage (comprehensive and collision), then the state will require that you have at least liability coverage. Part of the basic auto coverage package is medical and uninsured motorists. These two portions of a liability package can be excluded with your signature on a form in some states. However, this is not advisable, because the savings are minimal. More important, in the event of an accident where the other person is at fault and doesn't have insurance, your auto and medical expenses will be covered.

Additional discounts. There are oftentimes tons of discounts on your homeowners policy and especially your automobile policy that are yours for the asking. For homeowners, you can get discounts for a security system, tile roof, fenced yard, nonsmoking household, gated community, or enclosed garage. For automobile policies, ask for discounts for driver's ed, safe driving records, security systems on a car, an enclosed garage, nonsmoker policy, drivers aged thirty to sixty, multicar discounts, or military discount. Purchasing auto and homeowners from the same company will also sometimes qualify you for special discounts.

For a special section on "everything you wanted to know about life insurance," just e-mail assistant@elliekay.com and mention the code LIFE101. We will send you the necessary log-in information so you can access this part of the www.elliekay.com Web site for free. It's our way of saying thank you for buying this book.

A quick note about health insurance: With the health care bill that was recently passed by Congress, there will be a number of changes to health insurance. So to keep from becoming too quickly outdated, I've avoided discussing it here. However, if you want some tips on saving on your health insurance, check out my book *The Little Book of Big Savings* for a run-down on ideas and issues to avoid.

Buying a Car

The least expensive car for you to drive is probably the paid-for, older vehicle you are now driving! Go to chapter 4, "The 60-Minute Retirement and Savings Workout" for the plan on how to drive cars for free. People talk themselves into buying a car for a variety of reasons. Take, for example, gas mileage. When you actually calculate gas mileage and the money

you supposedly save—compared to interest payments and depreciation—
you will find that you do not even come close to saving money. The average new car depreciates roughly 25 percent to 30 percent within the first
eighteen months, with an average loss of value of $6,000 as soon as you
drive it out of the parking lot.[1] So look for a used vehicle before you consider buying new.

But when interest rates are mind-bogglingly low or a family needs
the warranty (because of high mileage), it may be best to get a new car. Try
to get an end-of-the-year clearance model, a demonstrator model, and if
possible, buy it in December or January—the leanest months in the car-
selling industry. The following tips can apply to buying a car new or used.
Negotiate these three sales points separately:

1. **Price.** Negotiate the price of the car at a dealership apart from
   the value of your trade-in. Tell the salesperson you want to determine the price of the car without a trade-in. The reason you want
   to do this is because sales will oftentimes give you far more for
   your trade than you expect—thus hooking you on the deal.
   However, they discount the price accordingly—giving you less of
   a discount because of the additional amount they've put into
   your trade. Look up the value of your car at www.edmunds.com,
   print out the page, and take it with you to the car lot.

2. **Trade-in.** Now that you've determined the price of the car, ask
   what the dealer will give you on your trade. Most honest dealer-
   ships will tell you that you will get more for your car if you sell it
   yourself. A little elbow grease and some topnotch detailing can
   net you hundreds of dollars more than a dealer will give you. But
   military families don't always have the time to do this due to
   moves, temporary duty schedules, and courses. To determine the
   value of your car, go to www.edmunds.com. Not only does
   Edmunds car-buying guide list new-car prices, used-car prices, car
   comparisons, and car buying advice, but it also gives car ratings,
   car values, and auto leasing information. Print out the page listing

your car and take it with you to the dealership. Or you could try the Kelly Blue Book site at www.kbb.com. Make sure you see the paperwork in advance of any vehicle that is said to be a certified preowned (CPO) vehicle, as there is a value attached to a vehicle that has passed all inspection points to be a CPO vehicle.

3. **Financing.** The finance and insurance office is where the lion's share of a dealership's profit is made. In this office, you will have to navigate interest rates, payments, terms, and warranties. Unless you put miles on your car for business or are a long-distance commuter, the extended warranties are usually not a good value. Also, you can generally do better on interest by selecting your own creditor, and the credit life insurance they offer is more expensive than raising your regular insurance premium by $20,000 to cover this expense.

Fuel Savings

It pays to shop around for gas. I'm amazed that gas stations within a mile of one another can charge upward of a ten-cent-a-gallon difference. That adds up! Here are some ways to save money through strategic gas mileage checks.

Tires: Check and change. The National Highway Traffic Safety Administration estimates that 55 percent of vehicles have at least one underinflated tire.[2] By maintaining the right amount of air in your tires and taking a few minutes to change the air filter, you can increase your gas mileage by 13.2 percent.

Strategize and slow down! Map out your vacation road trip by the cheapest gas along the route. Go to www.gaspricewatch.com or www.gasbuddy.com for pricing information. Get better mileage by taking the junk out of your trunk. Drive the speed limit. When you drive at 75 mph instead of 65 mph, you lower your fuel economy by 10 percent; driving 70 instead of 55 lowers it by 17 percent. The break-even point on running the air conditioner versus rolling down the windows for the best gas mileage is 40 mph. If you are driving more than 40 mph, then roll up the windows and enjoy the air conditioning, guilt free!

Gas prices. Go to www.gaspricewatch.com to find the best value for the best price and map your route accordingly.

Energy Savings

The latest report from the 2009 Consumer Expenditure Survey indicates that energy costs have risen 16.6 percent, which means the average American family will pay more than $3,600 this year in utilities.[3] Here are some simple ways to reduce energy usage and save money.

Time of use. Electricity is a big expense in the summer, and some states are offering a special discount for people who are willing to restrict their use of electricity during certain times of the day. It can be as simple as raising an air-conditioning setting and running swimming-pool pump motors at night. Check with your local power company for details.

Energy survey. Most utility companies also offer a free energy survey. Some regions will send out a surveyor; others offer the service via an online evaluation form. Since this is tailor-made for your home and utility usage, it's also the best way to target specific areas where you could save energy and save money. Go to your power company's Web site for more info.

CFL bulbs. Installing compact fluorescent light (CFL) bulbs is one of the easiest ways to start making an impact on your energy bills. Not only do you save money and energy, but you contribute to a cleaner environment by reducing fossil fuel usage. Modern CFL bulbs offer the following features and benefits:

- Use 75 percent less energy—saving you money.[4]
- Save more than $30 in energy costs over the life of the bulb.
- Last up to ten times longer.
- Operate at cooler temps, increasing indoor comfort.
- Produce the same attractive light as incandescent bulbs.
- Instantly start up and do not flicker or hum.
- Available in different sizes and shapes to fit almost any fixture.

CFL Recycling. CFL bulbs contain a trace amount of mercury, an essential element that allows them to be so efficient. Although this amount is extremely small and the mercury in one CFL bulb does not pose a hazard to you or the environment, there are millions of CFLs currently being used in households and businesses. It's important that everyone make an effort to keep large concentrations of fluorescent lighting out of landfills by taking burned-out bulbs to a local household hazardous waste facility.

Buy Energy Star–rated products. If you want to save up to 25 percent in energy costs, then look for the Energy Star rating on everything from hair dryers to small appliances and especially on larger appliances such as refrigerators. If your local store does not carry the Energy Star–rated product you want, don't let that stop you from buying green. Just go to the retailer's main Web site (for example, www.walmart.com) and look for the item of your choice, then select the "site to store" option where your item is shipped free to your local store for pickup. This not only allows you to pay the lowest price on your energy-efficient item, but it also saves the environment by reducing waste in terms of the extra packaging needed for conventional shipping. By doing our part, little by little, we'll find more green in our pockets and make a greener earth at the same time.

Food and Household Products

By following these tips, you can easily save 30 percent to 50 percent off your food bill:

Buy low. Try to never buy anything at full price, unless you have a coupon, which makes it a good value.

Watch for sale ads. Subscribe to your local paper so you can have the weekly sale advertisements delivered to your door each week. Or visit the grocery store's Web site.

Go high-tech. Use your smartphone to compare prices by going to the Web site that compares prices called www.retailmenot.com. Plus you can upload coupons to your phone and use them at the register. These are available at your grocer's Web site and at www.retailmenot.com.

Match values. Make out your shopping list according to what is on sale. Combine coupon values with sale items to determine if an item is worth buying.

Use coupons. By knowing your coupons, you also know which ones can be combined for greater savings. For example, a manufacturer's coupon (reimbursed by the manufacturer) can usually be used along with a store coupon (reimbursed by the store, such as Walgreens). The best resources for finding coupons are the freestanding inserts (FSIs) in your Sunday paper. Look on products, on pull boards attached to an aisle, and even electronic coupon dispensers in the store.

Research online. Check out sites such as www.couponmom.com and www.thegrocerygame.com. These are great sites that do the research for you by listing what is on sale in your area, what manufacturer's coupons are available, and what store coupons can be matched up for the best deals. Each week you'll find items that will cost only pennies or are free.

Shop with a list. If you shop with a list and stick to it (except for sales and other discounts), you will save close to 30 percent more than someone who doesn't.

Shop with cash. If you put cash in an envelope for the week, you will have a visual reminder of how much money you have left in your spending plan for the time period, so you are far less likely to overspend.

Save time in the store. People often tell me, "I don't have time to use coupons. I have a life!" Well, if you're organized, it only takes about two hours' work to use coupons effectively. To save time, use an aisle order chart (a map of the store, which you can request at the customer service desk) and make out your list according to aisle order.

Pull out as many coupons as you can at home and put them in a coupon envelope (a legal-sized envelope marked with the name of the store). Also, if you buy three or four copies of the Sunday newspaper and match up the FSIs, with one cut you can cut out four copies of the coupon at the same time.

Share. Once you've followed this system for a while, you'll find that you're getting tons of stuff free or for pennies. Consider sharing groceries with a local homeless shelter, women's crisis center, the Salvation Army, or even with a family up the street that has a need.

"Gently Used" Items

Consignment stores or garage sales are a way of life for people who want to cut costs, but these can also be a great source of making money, if you do it the right way. Here are the top ten tips for success when shopping for gently used items:

1. **Leave the kids at home.** We love our kids, but if possible, leave them home, and you'll do better. You'll be able to leave home at o-dark thirty, and you need to concentrate.

2. **Negotiate.** Don't pay more than you are comfortable with, but balance that with the fact that people have done a lot of work to make some extra money. I think the best rule of thumb is to ask yourself, *What am I willing to pay for this?* Then ask the seller if he'll take the lower amount you're willing to offer. If your price is reasonable, then eight times out of ten the seller will accept your lower price.

3. **Strategize your needs.** You need to develop a plan of action. First of all, think about the things you're looking for in a garage sale or consignment store and make a list. Categorize your clothing. Make a complete inventory. Get the right sizes for the people in your family. If you buy things too small, you're wasting money. Do you need a new bike for your son? Could you really use a good snow blower? Determine what you need to buy within the next two to three months and put the items on your list.

4. **Plan your route.** Get a newspaper with garage sales listings and a good city map. Note the start times and the items advertised in the notices. Prioritize the sales according to the advertised items

you need most, and plan your route accordingly. You may want to start in the area with the earliest openings. Visit all the sales in the same area to save time and money. Don't arrive much sooner than the set start time, because sellers won't have all their things set up yet, and they won't be in a negotiating mood that early in the day. The sales you visit later in the day are more likely to yield bargains as anxious sellers invite you to make an offer.

5. **Shop with a friend.** If you go with a friend, agree on the same strategy. If you can't agree, then go alone. Brenda Taylor was one of my all-time best garage sale buddies—she and I think alike! I really miss her. You probably won't have the time or energy to hit all the sales, so keep your trips to each house short and sweet. It might be a good idea to take along some coffee and snacks if you're going to be out for several hours.

6. **Don't buy what you don't need.** Unlike grocery shopping, I don't buy gently used items unless my family has a specific use for them. It isn't saving if you're just shopping. A good garage sale, consignment store mind-set is to buy only the goods you are going to have to buy anyway. If you find a pair of winter tights still in the original packaging and in your size and the seller is only asking for a quarter, then buy them. Instead of paying $4 for those at Wal-Mart, you've just saved $3.75! If you'll never wear those tights because they're two sizes too small, then you've wasted twenty-five cents.

7. **If it's broken, don't buy it!** People have garage sales or take items to consignment stores for different reasons. Everything on their tables and hanging in their awnings is there for a reason. Sometimes the reason is it's broken. So if you can't plug it in, put a battery in it, or start it, don't buy it, because it's probably broken. Life is too short to buy things you need to repair—unless you know what you're doing.

8. **If it's stained, leave it.** You can afford to be choosy at garage sales. If it's dirty and can easily be washed, buy it. If it's stained or you can't tell, leave it on the table. There are quality products for sale at garage sales that are in great shape. You don't have to settle for second-rate goods. Look for clothing with sales tags still on them and products in their original packaging.

    Check the zippers, buttons, and snaps on clothing. Pick and probe gadgets to make sure they work well. Count the accessories to a game to ensure all the pieces are there. Look pottery over carefully for nicks and dings. Check the knees on jeans to determine wear and tear. Look at the size on a curtain opening to make sure you have the right size curtain rod. It's not a bargain to buy $5 curtains when you have to pay $25 for a custom curtain rod to hang them!

9. **Check out newlywed sales.** I love newlywed sales. They have wedding gifts they didn't like or cannot yet appreciate still in the original boxes. Or they have duplicate toasters, microwaves, and coffee makers. My garage sale/consignment store buddy, Brenda, bought a new coffee grinder for $2 at one of these sales. Regularly, we pick up brand-new silver, crystal, and china at newlywed sales and keep them on hand for hospitality gifts, wedding gifts, or even an occasional birthday gift. There's absolutely no difference between paying $45 for a silver chafing dish at Sam's and paying $8 for the same piece, still in the box, at a yard sale— except for the $37 savings.

10. **Don't forget estate sales.** These offer many bargains, especially on antiques. Check the appliances carefully at these sales, though, as they tend to be well worn, older units. But if you know what you're looking for, you can find a diamond among the coal.

    If you live near a university that has family housing, you can find some great deals at yard sales. At the end of each semester, especially in May, families sell off household goods they can't take with them. It's worth a peek!

Hit the wealthy neighborhoods. Most of these people have never been to a yard sale and don't know how to price their items. If anything, they tend to price things lower than other yard sales, because they don't know common prices—or they don't care. If an item is overpriced, you can comment, "I usually find shoes like these for $2 at most garage sales." They will often give it to you for the lesser amount. It's a great way to get name brands. I've even found a few Neiman Marcus labels at these sales!

11. **Know the different kinds of garage sales.** There are two basic kinds of garage sales. The first kind is where *they want to get rid of stuff,* and the second is where *they want to make money.* When we lived in the military, we saw a lot of the first kind of garage sales—they were my favorite. These kinds of sales have things priced to sell or even give away. Military families move a lot and have only a certain weight allowance. They have to trim the extra fat and get rid of the things they can't use.

I'm not as fond of the second kind of garage sale, where they want to make money. I don't like those kinds of garage sales and never stay long. Most of the stuff is overpriced for a garage sale, and the folks become defensive if you ask them to take less. There are too many good sales out there to waste time at an overpriced garage sale. The irony of these two types of sales is that the first kind makes more money by moving more volume than the second.

12. **Stay on budget.** Garage sales need to be a part of your monthly budget. We usually budget $50 a week. This covers even the major garage sale purchases. The garage sale benefit, however, greatly diminishes if you go over budget in an effort to save money. It defeats the purpose of shopping these sales. If you're

given to impulse buying, then leave your checkbook and wallet in the car. While you're walking back to your vehicle to get your money, you'll have time to think about your purchase and decide whether you really need the item or not.

Garage sale and consignment shopping is fun! I go out for two or three hours and come back with $300 worth of merchandise for which I paid $30. Let's see, that's a savings of $270. Divided by three hours, that's a savings rate of $90 per hour. There's a psychological boost involved in the savings game and in seeing how we can save in the little ways.

Whatever your motivation for saving money, you've seen from this chapter that it doesn't have to be painful. In fact, it can be downright fun. It's a good idea to read some of this information with your spouse so you'll be in agreement when you start doing things that may appear to be out of the ordinary, like coming home with twelve bottles of shampoo (which you got for free!). You'll create a brighter future for your family by paying attention to the little expenses in life. Otherwise, these little things can add up to big debts that will only bring stress and strife to you and your spouse.

Remember: a penny saved is *more* than a penny earned!

☑ The 60-Minute Cha Ching Guide to Paying Less Workout Tip Sheet

1. Make-Up-Your-Mind Warmup (5 minutes)
- Say something positive about the results of the pretest or otherwise.
- Select a topic where you want to save money.
- Commit to following through on cutting costs and deciding where to put the savings.

2. Strength Training (10 minutes)
- Write down the results of the pretest.
- List a means of overcoming obstacles indicated on the pretest.

3. Cardio Burn (20 minutes)
- Read the detailed notes on your section of choice.
- Determine your previous costs by using past bank statements or bills.
- Do some research on how to save money and cut costs in your section.

4. Take Your Heart Rate (20 minutes)
- List a step-by-step plan and implement it.
- Implement measures to funnel the money you save into specific purposes.

5. Congratulations Cool Down (5 minutes)
- Say something positive about your progress today and/or about your spouse.
- Set the time and topic for your next workout.

7

The 60-Minute Travel and Fun Guide Workout

Part of the joy of raising children is to be a witness to each phase of their lives. When all the kids were at home, we took family vacations and had all sorts of fun together—an investment I do not regret. Now that they are growing up, one of the ways I've sought to stay in touch with the kids at home and the kids abroad is through social media sites such as Facebook and Twitter. One of the most revealing aspects of Facebook has been the revelation of my children's relationships. In fact, I was in Katterbach, Germany, a couple of months ago. When I checked in on Facebook, I found out that Jonathan, our sixteen-year-old son, was "in a relationship."

Instantly, I received messages from Daniel, Philip, and Bethany asking me about Jonathan's "relationship." In our family, we like to be involved, and to be honest, our school-aged kids aren't allowed to be in a relationship without Bob and me being in the know. The older kids knew this pit of Kay Kulture, and they knew their younger brother was out of bounds, which is why I had messages from them asking, "Say what?"

I was in Germany to give a critical message to an important group of military families whose spouses were being deployed into harm's way. It wasn't a lightweight, tourist trip, and the responsibility of what those people needed from me was a heavy mantle to carry. The last thing I needed was to be worried about Jonathan's being in a relationship.

But such is the nature of young love…or in this case, a young crush.

Another time one of my older sons commented on his girlfriend's post about how she was "running around like a chicken with my head cut off." To which he commented, "Ah, yes, but a very cute chicken." To which Jonathan commented, "Ahhh, gawwwh, you've got to be kidding!" To which Bethany commented, "Ah, that's sweet."

Yes, Facebook is the way to keep up on my children and their relationships. But it doesn't mean we've completely given up on family travel and vacations together. With our kids now scattered around the world, Bob and I have to be creative about how we accomplish those travel dreams.

How do you stay in touch with your kids? Do you take family vacations and prioritize family fun? What are your travel dreams? If you go into credit card debt or leverage the equity in your home to pay for that trip, then your dream can have an untimely end in a nightmare of bills and blues. But never fear, thanks to a recovering tourist industry, you can make your dreams come true, debt free.

Preworkout Quiz

1. In ten years will this [lifestyle, entertainment, fun, vacation, etc.] matter more than having the freedom of being debt free?
2. Is this travel and fun a family investment or a personal indulgence?
3. What is really important to me? to my spouse? to my kids?
4. How does spending money on travel and fun help me to reach my financial goals?
5. What will I remember most about my kids when I'm retired and they are grown?
6. What will my kids remember most about their childhood when they are grown and rearing my grandchildren?
7. Can I pay cash for this vacation? If I can't, will I still take it?

The 60-Minute Travel and Fun Guide Workout

1. Make-Up-Your-Mind Warmup (5 minutes)

This chapter's pretest was a little more reflective and more subjective than other pretests. So spend a few minutes meditating on the questions. Then say something positive about the results of the pretest or otherwise. Select the category you will concentrate on in this workout in the area of fun, entertainment, and travel. Commit to learning about and implementing new ways to pay less.

2. Strength Training (10 minutes)

Write down the results of the pretest and use it as a guide to this workout, especially as to how much money you will spend and how you can stay on budget or pay cash and still have fun. List any obstacles, as well as a means of overcoming them, as indicated on the pretest. Consider including not only financial or time obstacles, but also the materialistic or subjective roadblocks that can derail your resolve.

3. Cardio Burn (20 minutes)

Read the detailed notes for your chosen category, placing checks next to the tips that hold the most appeal to your situation. Develop a time line to implement your fun or travel plan. For example, if you are going on a vacation, map out how long it will take to pay cash for the trip and establish the time line accordingly. Determine and list the costs for this category or spending amounts.

    Save your results and paperwork in your pocket folder.

4. Take Your Heart Rate (20 minutes)

Implement your plan and print out any documentation for your pocket folder. Delegate responsibilities to other family members and set into motion your first steps to travel, entertainment, and fun. Write down a step-by-step plan to save money in this category and track your savings.

5. *Congratulations Cool Down (5 minutes)*
Say something positive about your progress today and/or about your spouse. Set the time and topic for your next workout.

Travel and Fun Categories

Vacations
One of the reasons many families overspend on vacations is because of a failure to plan ahead. They arrive at their destination and decide to take in several unplanned tourist attractions. They eat at specialty restaurants and buy overpriced souvenirs that will end up in next year's garage sale. This failure to plan ahead costs hundreds, if not thousands, of extra dollars each year.

Set a budget before you pull out of your driveway. Decide what activities take priority and *stay on budget.* Each family member can contribute ideas and decide on a plan that will accommodate as many interests as possible. For example, your hubby wants to go to the new water park at your selected camping spot, but you want to go to the amusement park. The water park costs just as much as the amusement park, and you can't do both. Suggest a trip to the nearby beach for one day (since you have no beaches near your home) and a trip to the amusement park for another day. It's a good compromise, and you're still within your budget.

Estimate the cost of meals, gas, and incidentals. Try planning your vacations during off-seasons, if possible. You'll save significantly on everything from hotel rooms to area attractions.

Select vacation areas in your locale. Since we always moved so much, we tried to see everything there was to see within our area. We made day trips to area sites and saved the cost of a hotel room. We packed lunches and had a great time relaxing at roadside picnic tables while the kids ran wild.

Here are some other less expensive vacation ideas:

Working vacation. Instead of paying $1,000 for a family of four to spend a week at a gorgeous camp in the Colorado Rockies, you can have a working vacation for free, with plenty of time for family. Some campgrounds offer this kind of trade-off. If your family enjoys this kind of environment, it would be worth your time to contact a local retreat center or campground.

Learning vacation. Some of these vacation packages are education based. Shaw Guides (www.shawguides.com) offers trips that match families with learning vacations around the world. Exploritas, which was formerly called Elderhostel (www.exploritas.org), offers people fifty-five and older up to ten thousand options, starting out with programs under $600.

Volunteer in the wild. Wilderness Volunteers (www.wildernessvolunteers.org) is a nonprofit organization created in 1997 that offers people of any age a chance to maintain national parks, forests, and wilderness areas across the United States. Everything from trail maintenance to re-vegetation projects are on the agenda. Participants provide their own camping gear and share campsite chores. Most Wilderness Volunteer trips last about a week and provide a lifetime's worth of memories.

Military family vacation. If you are a military family or a veteran, you can save even more money through the Armed Forces Vacation Club. Sign up at www.afvclub.com, which allows you to book time-share-type condominiums and accommodations for only $250 per week. The club at Oahu, Hawaii, was absolutely gorgeous and was situated on some of the most expensive real estate in the world: Waikiki Beach! Be sure to book early for popular locations. But if you're prepared to visit less touristy areas, you can book as little as one week in advance.

Rent someone else's vacation home or time-share. Whether you're looking for a cabin in Colorado, an adobe in Arizona, or a lake house in Louisiana, you'll find these rental properties at Vacation Rentals by Owners (www.vrbo.com). Unlike a home-swapping situation, you are actually renting someone's vacation home or time-share for the week. The Web site has photos, rates, and detailed descriptions for all fifty states. If you visit the ski places in the summer and the beach places in the winter, you can save even more. For example, a ski lodge in Park City, Utah, rents a 2,100-square-foot, two-bedroom unit for $1,700 in the winter and only $286 in the summer!

Theme park vacations. Packages have long been a way to maximize your savings at Disney, and "Magic Your Way" tickets offer price reductions for theme park tickets. You can decide whether staying on or off the property is a better value, but note that staying at a Disney property provides perks like complimentary airport shuttles and luggage delivery. In addition to the Disney sites, check out unofficial Web sites such as www.mousesavers.com, www.themouseforless.com, and www.allearsnet.com.

For other theme parks, go to www.amusementpark.com and www.themeparkinsider.com, which cover information on seventy theme and amusement parks worldwide. The reader opinion section rates parks on a 1-to-10 scale for attractions, restaurants, and hotels.

Don't forget to check the theme park's own Web site for details. You don't need to buy at the gate when you can get the tickets cheaper online or with another promotional offer (such as buying tickets at a local grocery store, bringing in a soft-drink can for a discount, etc.). Some human resources departments at larger companies offer discounts, so be sure you and your friends or family check with their employers first. Almost all morale and welfare (MWR) offices of military agencies offer discounted tickets for military personnel and veterans. Student unions might also offer discounted tickets.

Disneyland will offer discounts for locals if you show proof of a California-area zip code. Sometimes, you might have to purchase these tickets at a local grocery or drugstore, so go to their Web site for more details.

You can use your membership in the American Automobile Association (AAA), AARP, or warehouse club memberships to score discounted tickets. Some airlines and hotels, such as Hilton and Marriott, will even let you trade frequent traveler points for tickets.

Some theme parks like to push three- to five-day passes, and unless you and your kids are theme park nuts with a healthy disposition, you are not going to get the full benefit of that ticket. So don't overbuy. Parents with preschoolers are going to find that one day at any park will be enough because (1) children's tolerance level for overstimulation is low and they just get tired and (2) so many rides are off-limits to preschoolers, so you can pretty much do it all several times in a day.

Our family has been to dozens of theme parks over the years, and we've held Six Flags Magic Mountain season passes for the last three. We have found great ways to get the most for our dollars. Here are our top ten tips:

1. **Bring your own bottles.** While you cannot take food into a theme park, you can take water bottles that may be refilled at will. You don't need expensive sodas, sugary lemonade, and frozen ices to whittle away your food dollars. Your body and your wallet need water.

2. **Bring your own food.** If you are driving or your hotel room is nearby, pack your lunch in a cooler and take a break to save $75 or more on lunch. Be sure you get your hand stamped so you can reenter the park and enjoy!

3. **Use coupons.** When you're searching the Web sites, be sure to pick up any coupons that might be offered by those sites, your hotel, or as part of your ticket purchase. These coupons are often good at restaurants within the theme park and can add up to big bucks.

4. **Choose filling items.** Many theme parks carry fresh fruit for $1 a fruit (versus $5 for a pink thing ice cream treat), and they are a healthier, cheaper option. Turkey legs at Magic Mountain and Disney are usually around $5 and can fill up more than one person—plus they are portable, so you can eat while you're in line.

5. **Order à la carte.** Most parks offer combo meals, but they do not advertise that you can usually save by ordering the meal without the sides (or the drink—since you have your water!).

6. **Give kids an allowance.** We always give our kids a budget for the park. What they do not spend, they get to keep. They can spend money on food or souvenirs or save it. While they will buy some food (that's a requirement), they can choose healthier, cheaper options to maximize their budgets.

7. **Buy at the end.** Don't allow kids to purchase souvenirs until the end of the day. This helps to eliminate impulse purchases, and it keeps you from having to rent a locker for the goods and/or tote them around all day.

8. **Buy online.** You don't have to buy a Disney shirt at Disney. Before you go to the park, go online to www.overstock.com or www.graveyardmall.com for discounted, theme park–related merchandise and tuck these goodies in your suitcase to spring on the kids when you get there. If you're headed to a Disney park, check out www.disneyoutlet.com. This online retailer recently advertised Disney princess and Buzz Lightyear sweatshirts for kids for just $5.99.

9. **Refills.** There are often refill options for drink bottles that you purchase at the park. The refills are usually 25 percent of the cost of a regular drink. This is an option for those who don't want to drink water all day and want the splurge of an ice-cold lemonade slushie on a hot afternoon. (Sounds good to me right now!)

10. **Pool your resources.** Even if your kids have their own budgets, they can purchase items together for a discount. For example, if one child wants the side dishes on a combo meal and another wants the main course, they could purchase the combo and split the difference for a savings. This same technique works for purchasing multiple souvenirs when there is a multipurchase discount offered.

Dude Ranches. Think of the movie *City Slickers* and expand that idea into the new millennium. These days, dude ranches are all about white-water rafting, big-name chefs, Pilates classes, and, yes, horses. You can go to www.ranchweb.com as your best source to find the best value on dude ranches. You can search by location, rates, or activities. There are ranches such as HorseWorks, Wyoming, which offers cattle drives, and places like Montana's Lone Mountain Ranch, where you can do yoga before your morning ride. Elk Mountain Ranch in Colorado is one of the many ranches with extensive programs for young children. Dozens of dude ranches offer fly-fishing and mountain biking, but horsemanship remains the big draw. Some of these even have rock climbing, birding, and environmental lectures. A single price covers all meals, riding, accommodations, and many activities. These start as low as $700 per person per week.

A trip to the Holy Land. It's important to compare package deals and tour values by going to a comparison site such as www.travelzoo.com. In some cases, you actually pay more money to go to Israel with a celebrity than you would if you go on your own. Remember that most group packages raise enough money to pay for several guest coordinators to attend at no cost, because your tour prices cover these.

To save money, go to www.goisrael.com and do as much planning as possible. Stay in a hostel, guesthouse, or a kibbutz, which comes with a free breakfast. Buy a pass for all national parks to save as much as 35 percent on the most popular attractions.

Air and Hotel
Airfares. Check out the fares on the Internet, such as www.bookingbuddy.com, which will check more than 140 sites, including the popular ones, such as www.travelocity.com, www.webflyer.com, www.orbitz.com, www.bestfares.com, www.expedia.com (or 1-800-397-3342), www.smartliving.com, and www.cheaptickets.com.

Moment's Notice is a booking specialist (www.moments-notice.com or 1-888-241-3366). They charge an annual fee of $25 but boast bargain basement prices and some of the best values for cruises, Europe, Rio de Janeiro, and certain parts of the Caribbean. Sometimes if you buy a red-eye special for substantial savings, you can show up at the ticket counter early and see if they can schedule you out on an earlier flight.

Travel Zoo. Subscribe to the "Weekly Top Twenty" at www.travel-zoo.com to get the late-breaking deals on airfares, hotels, packages, entertainment, and much more. Bob and I have used this alert to get deals to Ireland, New York City, Greece, show tickets, and much more for an average of 30 percent below retail.

Online auctions and Priceline. It seems that online auctions on the Internet will survive because people are getting good bargains and are willing to continue to use these services in order to get and sell the trips they want. Online auction sites for airline tickets and other travel needs tend to be low on service but high on value. Look for established sites such as www.ebay.com, www.priceline.com, www.skyauction.com, and www.bidtripper.com for some good values. You can get half-priced hotel rooms, rental cars, plane tickets, entertainment tickets, etc. You will need to do some research on the balance of a good airfare with a good hotel rate. For example, even though airfare to Chicago can be cheap (they have two major airports that are served by dozens of airlines), city hotel costs can be steep. Finding a cheaper hotel at an auction and the airfare at a travel site could be the best value.

Hotels. You can often find package deals for great hotel rates at an airline Internet site when you book travel. You can also find great rates on car rentals when you're booking these other services. I've found that sometimes I'm getting an even better rate at www.southwest.com on hotels and rentals than I would get by bidding on a room or car at www.priceline.com. Plus those bookings are reflected on my Southwest miles as well, earning me free trips. So when you're checking airline fares (see the previous paragraph), be sure to check the hotel and rental rates as well.

In addition to some of the auction sites already mentioned, you can also check hotel sites for weekly Internet specials, such as www.quikbook.com and www.1800usahotels.com. Try the following for e-mail alerts: Hyatt at www.hyatt.com, Radisson at www.radisson.com/hotdeals,

Holiday Inn at www.basshotels.com/holiday-inn, Best Western at www
.bestwestern.com, and Hilton at www.hilton.com. Don't be put off by the
first price you see; look specifically for hotel details. For example, at
Hilton.com I've frequently found the indication, "Prices start at $230,"
only to find that with my AAA and military discounts, I can get the same
room for $116. Plus those online bookings count toward my frequent
stayer points, and those translate into free hotel nights.

For last-minute hotel rooms, you could go to Priceline.com and click
on the Pricebreaker Deals tab for the latest in great values.

Phone calls while traveling abroad. Consider signing up for Skype
(www.skype.com). You can set up an account at this Internet site and talk
to anyone almost anywhere for about a penny a minute. You can add to
the experience if you have a Webcam or a headset. If the people you are
calling also have Skype, then you can talk for free. If not, then you can go
on the Skype account and call any number in the world for pennies. We've
started using this service to talk to friends, family, and clients in Israel,
China, New Zealand, Australia, and Hawaii.

Entertainment

Life's simple pleasures truly are the best. We can learn to enjoy and find our
entertainment in the simple things. We can even find relaxation in productivity. Make a list of what you consider entertainment, and try to practice those things on the list that don't cost much but yield high personal
satisfaction. Then when you spend money to take a vacation, you will
come back feeling more satisfied, rather than feeling like you have to start
planning your next expensive trip to find contentment. Here are some
ideas for starters:

Day Trips. It's been said that "change is as good as rest." So get out
your map and look at day trips in your area. You may be surprised at how
many fascinating small towns are within a short drive from your home.
There will be lots of places you can enjoy visiting, such as historic build-
ings, architecture, gardens, markets, or antique stores.

Museum memberships. Museum memberships usually have a reciprocal list that can save you money locally and when you travel. We joined our local museum for only $50 a year and received an Association of Science Trade Centers (ASTC) passport. This passport allowed us access to hundreds of other museums, even though we only visited a dozen other museums on our trips in the last year. You can search just about every museum in the country by area if you go to www.astc.org.

Parks and open spaces. Few things are more romantic than a picnic in the park. If you have local public gardens or parks, make up a picnic lunch and soak in the scenery.

Hiking is also a great way to combine exercise with together time. Discover the countryside around you. You'll be amazed at what's at your doorstep. Use the search term "hiking trails" on the Internet for a multitude of ideas. For a complete "what, when, where, and how" of hiking and walking, go to www.sierraclub.org/outings. Or for a full listing of national parks, go to www.nps.gov/parks.html. If you are a member of AAA, check out www.aaa.com for tried-and-true vacation sites. For state searches of hundreds of leisure activities on federal lands, go to www.recreation.gov.

The library. Your local library is a great source of entertainment. You can borrow DVDs, audio books, CDs, audio cassettes, travel guides, *Consumer Report* magazines, as well as ever popular books. Many libraries offer free classes and guest lectures. Try researching your family tree at a library with a good genealogy reference section.

Games. You know all those games you got the kids for Christmas and birthday presents? They're just taking up space on a shelf when they could be a great source of entertainment for your family. When surveys tell us the average amount of spouse-to-spouse and parent-to-child time is measured in minutes, we know that game playing isn't the only thing we may be missing in life.

Sports and exercise. Killing two birds with one stone is one of my favorite pastimes. Bob and I like to take a walk and talk while we are exercising the puppies. It accomplishes two important functions: we exercise our legs and jaws for all two-footed and four-footed creatures involved. Basketball, soccer, baseball, and jogging are all inexpensive and fun sports to participate in as a family.

Camping. According to a recent survey, the most common denominator in individuals who expressed a satisfying childhood is camping.[1] The family that plays together stays together, and this is especially true in the great camping adventure. But before you take the big plunge and buy a camper, tent trailer, or motor home, consider renting a camper for a weekend. At www.rvrental.com, we found rentals across the country that ranged from $117 a day to $385 a day. Depending on the owner of the recreational vehicle (RV), other charges to consider are hospitality kits, kitchen kits, and/or emergency road kits. Cleaning fees will apply if the RV is not returned in the same condition in which it was rented.

Backyard camping. If you're looking at tent camping and you're not quite sure your family will appreciate it—or if you're just plain chicken to try it out—then practice in your own backyard. Pitch a tent for the kids the first night, so they can have the experience of sleeping in the great outdoors. Buy a mini-firepit and make your own s'mores. Tell scary or silly stories around the campfire. When my family and I sit around a campfire, we love to quote one-liners from our favorite movies while everyone tries to guess which movie they're from.

You're going to need some camping gear. Some of the best places to get your equipment are garage sales and thrift shops, such as Play It Again Sports. Make sure the items work and all the parts are there. If you want to invest in camping gear with another family, it would cut your costs in half and you would need to alternate camping dates.

Dining Out

Eating out with your family can be costly, siphoning thousands of dollars from your budget. So make a plan to never (or at least rarely) eat out and pay full price. Here are some ways you can save while dining out.

Coupons. Many mainline restaurants offer great coupon values through the Sunday newspaper coupon inserts. They can add up to 50 percent off the bill, or almost $400 per year! Online is another great place to find coupons. On my Web site at www.elliekay.com, I have links to coupon sources such as www.valpak.com that find local coupon values based on your zip code, or you can go to www.coolsavings.com, where they will e-mail you information on great deals.

Newspapers. Quickly scan the Living or Entertainment section of your newspaper for weekly restaurant specials on specific days. It may require going out on a Tuesday instead of a Wednesday. What only takes about twenty seconds to check can save you $20 or more.

Restaurants' Web sites. Find your favorite restaurant's Web site and check out their values. Many sites offer printable coupons as well as weekly specials. Try looking under www.[favorite restaurant's name].com, for example, www.bennigans.com.

Restaurant.com. This site (www.restaurant.com) lists more than six thousand eateries in twenty-five major metropolitan areas. It issues gift certificates and coupons for a fraction of their value in the restaurant. For example, I picked a favorite café where I paid $10 at the site for a coupon worth $25 toward my bill—a $15 savings for a restaurant where we were planning to eat anyway.

Two for one/One for two! If your fave place doesn't offer a buy-one-get-one-free special, then why not try the new trend of sharing a meal? This savvy approach is especially smart at a restaurant that's notorious for serving larger portions. You may have to pay a small surcharge for an extra plate, but your wallet (and waistlines) will thank you. Order water and save as much as 20 percent on the bill.

Entertainment books. These coupon books cost around $35 and are used as fund-raisers for nonprofit organizations, such as schools. Go to www.entertainment.com to find offers near you. Not only do they feature restaurant coupons, but they also offer great values on a variety of local and national services. But be forewarned: they're not cost-effective if you leave them at home!

School and community value cards. Many communities have fund-raiser cards that cost around $10 and are the size of a credit card. It's very easy to put these in your wallet and save with buy-one-get-one-free values, free drinks, desserts, and percentage-off values.

✔ The 60-Minute Travel and Fun Guide Workout Tip Sheet

1. Make-Up-Your-Mind Warmup (5 minutes)
- Say something positive about the results of the pretest or otherwise.
- Select the category (fun, entertainment, or travel) you will concentrate on in this workout.
- Commit to learning about and implementing new ways to pay less.

2. Strength Training (10 minutes)
- Write down the results of the pretest.
- List the obstacles indicated on the pretest and the means of overcoming them.

3. Cardio Burn (20 minutes)
- Read the detailed notes for your chosen category.
- Determine your previous costs for this category or spending amounts, and list them using past bank statements or bills.
- Research ways to save money in this category.

4. Take Your Heart Rate (20 minutes)
- Implement your cost-reduction plan and print out any documentation for your pocket folder.
- Write down a step-by-step plan to save money in this category and to track your savings.

5. Congratulations Cool Down (5 minutes)

- Say something positive about your progress today and/or about your spouse.
- Set the time and topic for your next workout.

8

The 60-Minute
Allowance Workout

"Badly done, Bethany! Badly done!" I glared at my sixteen-year-old daughter who had just made the dreaded mistake of assuming she could go out of town with her friends without asking permission.

She rolled her eyes, "*Emma,* right? Mom, would you stop quoting Jane Austen and let me know if I can go with my friends to Six Flags or not. I know I have to use my own allowance since it's a friend thing."

"Her character depends upon those she is with; but in good hands she will turn out a valuable woman," I said, quoting another line from the novel. I made eye contact, daring her to give me yet another eye roll.

Bethany stared back as if her life (or at least her fun) depended on it. "They *are* good friends, Mom. I know about value, because you trained me to be smart in how I spend my money at a theme park. You know I'll be in good hands."

I knew I was going to let her go with the youth group to the theme park, but she didn't, so before granting permission, I gave her a parting Austen quote: "The real evils, indeed, of her situation were the power of having rather too much her own way, and a disposition to think a little too well of herself."

"Thanks, Mom. Now can I have seventy-five dollars?"

Sometimes, even Jane Austen cannot help.

Preworkout Test

Read each statement and answer true or false.

1. I had an allowance when I was growing up.
2. I believe in allowances because they teach money skills.
3. Allowances should not be tied to chores.
4. It's hard work to administer an allowance.
5. If my child can manage her allowance money, she has the skills she'll needed to manage her own budget when she grows up.
6. Even if you live on a very tight budget, you can still give your child an allowance.
7. Kids should not have to use their allowance to pay for family fun.
8. Different-aged children should get different allowance amounts.
9. You should make sure your child follows the 10/10/80 Rule for allowances.
10. Most children love getting an allowance if they have the option.

Scoring

If your answer was "true" to:

8 to 10 questions: You have a firm understanding of the purpose and function of an allowance.

5 to 7 questions: You understand the basics of an allowance.

4 or less questions: You do not have a clear understanding of the purpose of an allowance.

The 60-Minute Allowance Workout

1. Make-Up-Your-Mind Warmup (5 minutes)
Say something positive about the results of the pretest or otherwise. Commit to establishing an allowance for your child(ren).

2. Strength Training (10 minutes)
Write down the results of the pretest, put a star by the answers you marked as "false," and work on these areas. Determine why you answered false. If you answered false to question 1, that works slightly against your favor, as adults who never received an allowance as a child are far less likely to see the value in administering an allowance to their children. List a means of overcoming obstacles indicated on the pretest.

3. Cardio Burn (20 minutes)
Read the detailed notes on this section about the purpose and function of an allowance. There are a lot of notes, so jot down or highlight those that particularly apply to your children. Determine what your children's allowance amount will be, based on their age and the information in the text. Also define the boundaries for how the money is to be spent (or saved) and when you will pay the allowance.

4. Take Your Heart Rate (20 minutes)
Write down the details of your child's allowance and call him into the room to discuss it with him. If you have more than one child, discuss each child's allowance separately. When you meet with your child, make sure you maintain a positive setting; you want him to be excited about money matters, not threatened by them. Let your child know about the allowance/chores connection and the reality of discipline. Explain the purpose and function of an allowance to your child in age-appropriate terms.

5. Congratulations Cool Down (5 minutes)

Say something positive about your progress today and/or about your spouse and your children. Set the time and topic for your next workout.

Benefits of an Allowance

There are numerous benefits of giving an allowance to your children. Here are some.

Money management. The most obvious benefit of an allowance is that it gives children an opportunity to learn how to manage money.

Safe trial and error. When kids learn to manage their money while they're under our care, they have the freedom to fail in a relatively safe haven. While this doesn't mean that we bail them out, it does mean that we're on hand to help walk them through the steps that will lead them back to the road toward financial stability.

Self-worth building. An allowance can make children feel good about themselves. How do you feel when you're at the beginning of a paycheck? Your children will learn to feel good about the fact that they have some money of their own to manage. They'll feel even better when they learn to give freely, save diligently, and spend wisely.

Build consistency. This is the biggest problem for most parents: they start something with well-intentioned spurts but fail to keep it going. It's important to pay children their allowance on the same day of the week or month. This gives them something to look forward to and allows them to budget their needs and wants accordingly.

Budget understanding. An allowance should be included in your family's budget, and your children need to know this. It shows them that teaching them about money, through the use of their own allowance, is important enough that it ranks as part of the family budget. It also sends a message to kids about the importance of a budget, thereby priming the pump for the day you will help them develop a personal budget of their own.

Theirs alone. The money they receive is something that is theirs. They own it, and we help them learn to spend it wisely, according to the biblical principles of good stewardship. If we give them their own money and then refuse to let them spend it as they see fit, then the allowance is just an exercise in futility.

To give children an allowance and then tell them how to spend it is just more authoritarianism. Authoritarians make all the decisions for their children, including how the children should spend their allowance. The children learn nothing about handling money or accountability.

We have to create a climate where our children have the freedom to test their limitations, discover how money works, and learn in the process. Some of these lessons will be hard, but the children won't learn them if we continue to make all the decisions for them.

Responsibility and accountability. Allowances provide parents with an opportunity to tie in the two elements of responsibility and accountability so that our kids can learn both of these invaluable life skills. Accountability and responsibility are closely related, and both are vital life skills that will help keep our children out of a financial counselor's office when they're adults. Let's take a closer look at these two critical areas.

Responsibility

The main objective in implementing an allowance is to teach our children about responsibility.

Members only. I do not advocate giving a child an allowance because she is a living and breathing being—as if an allowance were an inalienable right. On the other hand, your child is a member of your family and, as such, has certain responsibilities. Because she's a member of the family with responsibilities, she should get an allowance.

Not payment for chores. There's a delicate balance between paying your child for chores and withholding a portion of an allowance for chores not done. Try not to tie allowances to chores. Doing so gives children the impression that they should be paid for all work, even cleaning up after themselves. Give them both chores and an allowance because they are part of the family.

Responsibilities on demand. In our family, we've trained our children that they are part of a larger whole: the family. As responsible members, they are required to give their parents the help they need. While they have specific chores that they are to do on a regular basis, that does not exclude them from other, nonpaying work. We've trained our kids to fold laundry, vacuum the carpet, rake the backyard, or do whatever the family needs to get done as their part in the family. This doesn't mean we're not willing to pay them occasionally for some of these jobs (if they're trying to earn money and looking to do extra work). But it does mean that they'll do some work without an expectation that they have to be paid to do it.

Not for cowards. Teaching these skills is not an easy task; it takes time and it takes a plan that is uniquely suited to your child's needs and your family's limitations.

An allowance based on a child's age is a good place to start. So unless you have twins, all your children will get different allowances. Their chores or responsibilities need to be age appropriate too. Let's look at some practical ways to teach both of these objectives in a positive way.

- **Younger Children.** Even a three-year-old can help set a table, carry dishes to the sink, and pick up his toys and clothes. As a four-year-old, he can begin to learn to make his bed with help, and by the time he's five, he's doing a fairly decent job of it. One of the primary chores Joshua did when he was five years old was to organize the shoe rack we kept in our garage (we don't wear shoes in our house). One day we heard a sharp cry from the garage. I went to see what Joshua was doing. All he could say was, "Look at that, Mama!" His brother Daniel had a few friends over, and there were four sets of tennis shoes that were sizes twelve, thirteen, fourteen, and fifteen, and there was no place for Joshua to put them on the rack!

- **Older Children.** The older a child is, the more responsibility she tends to have in the family and the closer she is to living on her own—when she will have to make all her financial decisions. When our oldest, Daniel, started to complain that he was doing the lion's share of the work around the house, we gently reminded him that he also had the most privileges and that these were associated with his heightened responsibilities.

Accountability

An allowance provides parents with the opportunity to teach their children how to properly handle money. They are afforded a chance to learn financial accountability—a lesson that most adults still need to learn. But part of accountability is letting our kids face the reality that choices have consequences.

Natural consequences. This is a great tool to teach our kids accountability. When our middle child, Bethany, first began receiving an allowance, she often had it spent before her payday was over. She'd see something in a store and spontaneously blow her money on a cheap toy that would be broken by the next day.

We decided to emphasize for her the consequences of her choices. When she saw a cool pencil she wanted at the store and asked us to buy it, here's how our conversation went:

"Sure, you can buy that. Just use your allowance."

She'd reply mournfully, "But I don't have any left…," letting her voice trail off in a sympathy-seeking whine.

I'd pat her blond curls and say, "Well, then, I guess we'll see about it next Sunday, when you get your allowance again."

This simple technique began to teach her the natural consequences of spending all her money the first day, and made her accountable for her own spending habits.

Conditional allowance. While our kids receive an allowance because they're a responsible part of our family, it doesn't mean that we place no conditions on their allowances. They have a responsibility to do their chores (even though they're not getting paid to do chores). So the big questions are: How do you get kids to do their chores? What if they don't do them?

This is how we raised our children and it really works.

1. Establish a healthy authority over your child.
2. Hold your children accountable for their actions.
3. Let reality be their teacher.
4. Use actions more than words.
5. Stick to your guns, but don't shoot yourself in the foot.
6. Relationships come before rules.
7. Live by your values.

Here's an example. When Bethany was ten years old, she decided she would rather comb her hair a gazillion strokes rather than make her bed. In the mad dash to leave the house for school, she repeatedly left this chore undone. When she got home from school, she skipped over to a friend's house—leaving her undone chore still undone.

This was an ideal opportunity for Mom to step in to deal calmly with the situation. I asked seven-year-old Jonathan (aka Sweetpea), to make his sister's bed and paid him fifty cents for the three-minute chore. He was delighted to earn some more money (which he was saving for an F-15 model airplane kit).

When Bethany returned home, I informed her of the situation: she didn't do her job, Jonathan did it for her, and I took fifty cents from her upcoming allowance to pay for his services.

This approach is not failure proof, but it was effective for us. It also kept us from going over the edge and losing our cool over undone chores, a lack of responsibility, and sloppiness. It seems to hurt kids all the more to see their money go to their siblings, and this plan went a long way in reducing the amount of forgetfulness, laziness, and rebelliousness that we saw in our kids.

✓ The 60-Minute Allowance Workout Tip Sheet

1. Make-Up-Your-Mind Warmup (5 minutes)
- Say something positive about the results of the pretest or otherwise.
- Commit to establishing an allowance for your child(ren).

2. Strength Training (10 minutes)
- Write down the results of the pretest.
- List the means of overcoming obstacles indicated on the pretest.

3. Cardio Burn (20 minutes)
- Read the detailed notes on this section about the purpose and function of an allowance.
- Determine what your child's allowance amount will be, what the boundaries are, when you will pay it, and who will be responsible for issuing payment.

4. Take Your Heart Rate (20 minutes)
- Write down the details of your children's allowances, and call each child into the room to discuss it with her or him individually.
- Let your children know about the connection between allowance and chores and the reality of discipline.
- Explain the purpose and function of an allowance to your children in age-appropriate terms.

5. Congratulations Cool Down (5 minutes)
- Say something positive about your progress today and/or about your spouse and to your child(ren).
- Set the time and topic for your next workout.

9

The 60-Minute Kid
Entrepreneur Workout

Our son Philip attends the U.S. Naval Academy, which attracts the best and the brightest in our nation. He would say he got there by concentrating on academics, athletics, community service, and leadership. But I say that he got there because he had a paper route as a nine-year-old. Yes, I'm convinced that Philip succeeded in direct proportion to the work ethic he developed in his youth. I think a person's work ethic is developed in a variety of ways: the ballet dancer who learns discipline as a youth, the academic who learns to study well, the athlete who spends hours in practice in order to letter in sports, and the child who gets a job of his own to learn how to earn money. It's one of the reasons we've encouraged our kids to work hard in school and to consider launching their own business, whether it's a baby-sitting service, a car-washing club, or a paper route.

Daniel had a job at Dairy Queen and developed such a good work ethic that he garnered two scholarships to the University of Texas at Arlington. He worked part time while in college, and as a result, he was able to graduate debt free. Bethany worked at Blockbuster while she was in high school and earned a scholarship to Moody Bible Institute in Chicago where she also had her first radio job on the college campus network. The next two kids in the long Kay Kid line of hard workers are lettering in sports at school, earning honor-roll grades, and also have jobs that will serve them well in the future.

Yes, a solid work ethic can never be underestimated. So developing this work ethic by helping your children find their passion at a young age is priceless.

Preworkout Test

Think through and answer the following questions.

1. Name the number of jobs you had from ages one to eighteen. List the kinds of work each of them entailed.
2. How did you feel about earning your own money?
3. Did you value items you bought with your own money more than items that were given to you?
4. Did you ever feel unsafe at a job you had as a kid?
5. Did you have to pay for necessities from your own money as a kid?
6. Did you save money from your own jobs as a kid?
7. Did you give away money from your own job as a kid?
8. Did you grow up with a strong work ethic?
9. Did you see a strong work ethic modeled by your own parents?
10. Did you have any role models among people associated with the jobs you had as a kid?

Results: This test does not have a scorecard like the other tests. Instead, it is designed to help you think about the kinds of work ethic values you were raised with, how they might impact your role as a parent, and what you would like to do differently. Go back through the questions and put a star by those that you want to pass on to your children and an *X* by those you wish to avoid.

The 60-Minute Kid Entrepreneur Workout

1. Make-Up-Your-Mind Warmup (5 minutes)

This is going to be a workout that you will call your child into at the midway point. So you may want to set up a time for this workout that will be good for your child, when she is rested as well. Say something positive about the results of the pretest. Commit to helping your child work through a kid entrepreneur job. It is going to require your direct supervision to keep her in the game, so make sure you that can commit to the job before you allow her to pursue it.

2. Strength Training (10 minutes)

No matter what your pretest is like, whether you had highly compassionate and involved parents or whether your family was dysfunctional, you can change the course of that history with the way you interact with your own children. You have a fresh chance to make a big difference. Write down the results of the pretest and pay special attention to the items you selected that you want to transfer to your children and those that you want to avoid. List the means of overcoming obstacles indicated on the pretest.

3. Cardio Burn (20 minutes)

Read the detailed notes on this section. Make a list of the safety rules that apply to your child. Put marks by the items you want to discuss with your child when you call him in for the next section. Have a quick glance at the jobs listed and check out the more detailed descriptions of each at my Web site, www.elliekay.com, to see which ones you think would appeal both to your child and to you (because you will have to supervise and follow through when he cannot).

4. Take Your Heart Rate (20 minutes)

Ask your child to join you. Go through the boundaries that are necessary for your child to have in place before you can allow her to launch her own business. Pay special attention to the safety issues and make sure your child understands. Go through the jobs listed in this chapter and on my Web site, www.elliekay.com, to find one she may like. Narrow it down to five likable jobs, and decide which are practical enough to launch as a home-based business for your kid entrepreneur.

5. Congratulations Cool Down (5 minutes)

Say something positive about your progress today and/or about your spouse and to your child.

Set the time and topic for your next workout.

Jobs for Kids

As long as you are willing to supervise your child's work, see to his safety when dealing with the public, and set appropriate boundaries for him, then allowing kids to earn money can be a fun and prosperous venture.

Here are some great ideas to help your kids raise their own cash while enjoying the benefits of earning, saving, and sharing. While some of these are not new ideas, I've gone to the trouble (mental agony of trial and error) to add some tips on how to do the job well and the areas of the particular job that need special attention.

Let your kids look over the list of job possibilities in this chapter, then e-mail assistant@elliekay.com and mention the code KIDJOBS. We will send you the necessary log-in information so you can access the job descriptions in greater detail on my Web site, www.elliekay.com. Ask each child to see which ones sound fun. I've written the job descriptions and details with a child reader and adult supervisor in mind. We've also started out with some tips for parents to ensure that your children's jobs are safe and to maximize the teaching benefit of the work.

Parental Tips Before the Kids Take the Job

It may be the kids' job, but parental involvement is essential for a variety of reasons. For one thing, if your children don't follow through with their work or if they do a lousy job, then it reflects poorly on your family and on you as parents. Safety is also a biggie—especially in today's culture. Here's a checklist for parents to review with their children before they accept a job.

Safety. Do you know the people your children are working for? Will your children ever be in their employers' homes? If your children are working for neighbors, and you prefer that your children work outside, then you need to give them strict instructions that they are not to go into a stranger's home—even to go to the bathroom or get a drink. If you aren't familiar with that neighbor, then your children can come home to take care of their essentials. Or you might want to have them buddy up with a friend to do some of these jobs.

When it comes to jobs that require special equipment, be sure your children understand safety issues for lawn mowers, edgers—even pool-cleaning equipment. If your children break someone's equipment due to improper use, then you (or your children) will need to pay for the repairs. So be sure they know how to operate the tools necessary for the job.

If your children ever feel uncomfortable on a job, then give them the freedom to come to you immediately with their concerns without fear of a scolding. It's far better to be safe than sorry when it comes to your children's well-being and the well-being of the employer's property.

Age-appropriate work. Do you remember any time in your life when you were given a task that was beyond your ability? How did it make you feel? Were you frustrated or confused? Did you want to give up? I'm not talking about the daily grind of parenting children or going through the "joys" of adolescence; I'm talking about the need to do a job that was not a good fit with your basic skills and abilities.

It's important that you try to match your child with a job that is appropriate for her age. A seven-year-old shouldn't be allowed to take a job walking a seventy-five-pound Saint Bernard—unless your seven-year-old is about five feet four inches tall and weighs one hundred and thirty pounds!

There's a difference between childish irresponsibility and a child's ability. It's your role to determine the differences in your children and their ability to adequately perform the task at hand. A mismatched job will only lead to frustration and a bad feeling about work. But there are some jobs that we don't think our kids can do, and they surprise us with their efficiency! The key is to supervise any work your child does if you're not sure of the age appropriateness of the job. Once the child shows you she can do it, then let her excel!

On-the-job training. All the areas we've listed below come with job descriptions and details on how to do the job well. But there's no substitute for experience. Before your child ventures out on a job for pay, have her practice at home. In exchange for the training you give on how to do the job well, you will get the free fringe benefits of a clean car, a weed-free flower bed, a freshly mowed lawn, sparkling windows, free baby-sitting, a clean garage—you get the idea.

Follow through. Don't allow your child to do any job that you are not committed to helping him follow through with. Just as I ended up throwing the boys' paper route on occasion (with the help of two small assistants), you will need to be prepared to baby-sit if your child gets sick at the last minute or find a satisfactory substitute.

If you have to finish a job because of your child's lack of responsibility or inappropriate behavior, then your child will pay you the *full* amount he receives for the job—even if he did half the work but didn't complete it. For example, when I had to throw Philip's paper route because he had an after-school detention, he had to pay me twice the amount of a normal substitution. It's one of those tough-love lessons that will be priceless in the long run (even if it's painful in the here and now).

Quality work. The boundaries you might want to establish before your children start to work are the standards required for the job. Quality work and excellence should be the standard for our work as parents, and it's a good standard for our kids' work too!

Part of this work quality will be demonstrated in on-the-job training sessions, while another large part of it will only develop as your children work for other people.

It's important to praise your children when they do a good job. It's also wise to stress how one good job leads to another referral, which leads to more work, which will culminate in a bottom line of more profits.

Nifty "Cash for Kids" Ideas

Below is an extensive list of potential jobs for your child entrepreneur. Look over the options and see which ones are the most interesting and doable for your child. Then e-mail assistant@elliekay.com and mention the code KIDJOBS. We will send you the log-in information so you can access the job descriptions in greater detail on my Web site, www.ellie kay.com. There you will find detailed descriptions of each job, along with tips on how to get started, what to charge, and creative ideas on how to get—and keep—customers.

    paper route
    rent-a-kid
    rent-a-kid management expansion plan
    car wash and wax
    window washing
    garage cleaning service
    baby-sitting service
    baby-sitters' club

plants for profits
bucket o' business
mail service
pet minders
pet minders expansion program
pet washers
pet walkers
pet contest judge
clothing consignments
lawn service
outdoor house cleaning
candy-maker's creations
leaf-raking service
pecan sales
storm cleanup
flier service
holiday gift certificate offerings
gift-wrapping service
mistletoe sales
mama's helper
valentine delivery
hot dogs and cool drinks stand
Make 'Em Laugh Clowns Inc.
glamour gals
snow-related job
snow buddies for rent

☑ The 60-Minute Kid Entrepreneur Workout Tip Sheet

1. Make-Up-Your-Mind Warmup (5 minutes)
- Say something positive about the results of the pretest or otherwise.
- Commit to helping your children work through a kid entrepreneur job.

2. Strength Training (10 minutes)
- Write down the results of the pretest.
- List a means of overcoming obstacles indicated on the pretest.
- List the items you want to reinforce with your children and those you want to avoid from the pretest.

3. Cardio Burn (20 minutes)
- Read the detailed notes on this section.
- Make a list of the safety rules that apply to your children.

4. Take Your Heart Rate (20 minutes)
- Ask your children to join you and go through the jobs listed to find ones they may like.
- Narrow it down to five likable jobs, and decide which are practical enough to launch as a home-based business.

5. Congratulations Cool Down (5 minutes)
- Say something positive about your progress today and/or about your spouse and to your children.
- Set the time and topic for your next workout.

10

The 60-Minute College Plan Workout

As you know, Bob and I have seven children.

Three have graduated from college.

Two are in college.

Two are headed toward college.

There is no college student-loan debt in the Kay house.

When people ask me how we are putting our kids through college debt free, the answer is multifold. First, we train our children from a young age that going to school, doing your homework, and getting good grades is their primary job. By teaching them a good work ethic, we are laying the groundwork for scholarships and more. Second, we send them to schools that we can afford or where they get the best scholarship offers to cover the most expenses. Third, we have saved a modest amount of college money to help them pay their room and board and, in some cases, partial tuition. Last, we require that they work part time in the summers or during the school year (through a work-study program or a regular job) to do their part to pay for college. By implementing these four disciplines, each of our children is set to graduate debt free. The kids who are going to college now have over a half-million dollars in scholarships, and if the last two stay true to their goals, our kids will have garnered more than a million dollars in scholarships by the time they are through with school.

The following workout is designed for you to do with your aspiring college student in order to decide where to go to college, how to pay for it, how to leverage an unconventional means of supplementing college expenses, and how to earn scholarships. The complete financial guide to saving for college through a variety of different investments (including 529 plans, Coverdell, etc.) is found in chapter 4, "The 60-Minute Retirement and Savings Workout." In this chapter, however, you'll be looking at other creative means of addressing the college issue.

Preworkout Test

Today's pretest will consist of a Q&A, where you get to be the expert who is preparing a student for college. These are actual Q&As that I wrote about in *Life: Beautiful* magazine.[1]

Questions

1. We have a child graduating from high school this year and want him to start out right with good credit scores. How does a teenager go about starting to build good credit?

    —Pam from San Francisco, California

2. I'm going to start college in the fall and my parents require that I pay for my own books. Do you have any tips to save money in this area?

    —Brittney from Crowley, Texas

3. Our twins are in their second year of college, and we've been paying tuition for over a year. Is there anything we might be overlooking in trying to find some ways to help pay for college? It's really difficult financially with two in college at once!

    —Marie from Quartz Hills, California

4. My husband and I want to help with our son's college expenses (he graduates in two years), and we don't want him to be saddled with huge student loans. Several of our friends and other family members have said, "Just take out a second mortgage or use the equity in your home to pay for college." What do you think about that?

   —Marty from Topeka, Kansas

Answers

1. On building good credit

I've launched two high school graduates in the past two years, and I know how important it is for them to have good credit. A good credit score will not only impact the interest rates they pay for a new car, but the scores also determine whether they pay a utility deposit, if they'll get a good job, and how much they may pay for their auto insurance.

First, they need to open their own checking and savings accounts near their college. Second, they should apply for a credit card with a low credit limit ($500 to $1,000). They can either apply for this at their bank or find a credit card provider at www.bankrate.com. Do not ever cosign for a credit card for your children, and make sure they have accountability for the use of their card so that they do not get into credit card debt. They should pay off their card each month, or they should make a commitment to cut up the card if they cannot pay it monthly. Our son Daniel started this way and has already built good enough credit scores by age twenty to prequalify for a modest homeowners loan. By starting small and paying consistently, your children can begin to build a good credit score.

2. On buying school textbooks

Buying your books from a used-book store can save money, but buying them online can save even more. One of my sons, a journalism major, needed a book that was $150 new and $30 at a used-book store. He found it for $1.50 at www.amazon.com. You can also try www.campusbooks.com to compare prices and find the best values across the Internet. Just be sure to buy them two weeks before classes start. As soon as you get your book list, begin your search, because the early bird gets the best value on books!

3. On ways to pay for college

It pays to keep looking for savings options even when you think you've exhausted all that is available to you. For example, you and your student should regularly visit the university's financial aid office, which is oftentimes a clearinghouse of information. They not only help students determine what loans they qualify for, but will also steer them to participating lenders who are offering the best terms and service. Parents can do their own assessment at www.collegeboard.com with their "Paying for College" Web-page calculator.

The Free Application for Student Financial Aid (FASFA) form is the first step in applying for aid. It includes (1) need-based guaranteed loans such as Stafford loans, which are variable and currently at 3.42 percent while Perkins loans are at a fixed 5 percent, (2) grants such as the Pell Grant and the Federal Supplemental Education Opportunity grant that each provide a gift of up to $4,050 per student per year, and (3) the Federal Work-Study program, which allows students to receive up to $2,000 per year, 25 percent of which is matched by the participating institution.

State loans and grants also are available. Your college or university financial aid office should be able to quickly assess your child's eligibility. Plus this office will also direct them to scholarship applications and programs for both new and current students.

4. On using home equity to pay for college

You should never borrow on your own future to pay for your children's future. In any discussion of college costs, it's important to keep your priorities straight. Your children's education shouldn't cost you your retirement. This means it's not a wise idea to take out a home equity loan, an equity line of credit, or refinance your mortgage in order to pay for school. This would reduce the amount of equity in your home, increase the risk of possible foreclosure, and incur costs in interest charges that may cost more if the term on the new mortgage is greater than the remaining term of the existing mortgage.

To finish this pretest, go back and reread the questions and answers. See how many of these answers line up with the actions you are already taking to prepare for college. Which question needs more of your attention? For example, are you seriously considering a home equity loan or line of credit to pay for your children's college or are there some alternatives you have not yet explored? Are your children paying for their own books? Look at ways to help your children find the best values. Have you ignored the entire idea of building your students' FICO score? Then concentrate on that area to help them to get started. Pick one area and address it this coming month.

The 60-Minute College Plan Workout

1. Make-Up-Your-Mind Warmup (5 minutes)
- Say something positive about the results of the pretest or otherwise. If you are working with a spouse or your college-bound student, encourage him or her at the beginning of this workout to set the tone in the next hour for achievement and success.
- Discuss what aspect of college planning you want to cover based on the topics that follow this section.
- Commit to establishing a workable plan for college.

2. Strength Training (10 minutes)
- Discuss the results of the pretest and why you agree or disagree with some of the answers.
- List the means of overcoming these obstacles as indicated on the pretest.

- Rephrase any negativity into a positive counterpart, such as "I know you won't get any scholarships" to "You might end up with a scholarship for something because there are all kinds of scholarships out there." Rephrase "There is no way we can do college with no student loans" to "If we explore some creative alternatives or even adjust our college expectations, we could do this with no further debt."

3. Cardio Burn (20 minutes)
- Read the detailed notes in the "First Things First" section and then the section you plan to cover in today's workout.
- If you haven't decided on a college, you may want to crunch the numbers involved in some of the options.
- If you haven't taken advantage of extra credit hours available to your student, you may want to set up a plan to capture those.
- If you are working with a spouse or child, then read the material out loud so that all of you have all of the information for the workout. Be sure to put any materials you fill out in the pocket folder marked "The 60-Minute College Plan Workout."
- Research or access online the materials you may need for the next section.

4. Take Your Heart Rate (20 minutes)
- Write down the specifics of the topic you are discussing.
- Delegate action steps for how you can make progress in this area today. If it's scholarships, then begin to find ones that meet up with your student's skills, involvement, and passion. If it's testing for College Level Examination Program (CLEP) hours, then order the study guide online.
- If you are crunching tuition numbers, then gather and print out as much data as you have available to you.

- Now is the time to delegate responsibilities for anything that cannot be accomplished in this one hour. This information will be brought back to the next college planning workout session. This is the section where you are putting action to your topic.

5. Congratulations Cool Down (5 minutes)
- Say something positive about your progress today and/or about your spouse, as well as your college student.
- Set the topic and time for your next workout.

The College Plan

First Things First

In any discussion of college costs, it's important to keep your priorities straight. You've got to leave yourself some money for retirement. How else can you afford that mechanical bull-riding lesson and those parasailing flights (been there, done that, *love* it!)?

I really believe that you, as a parent, should try to avoid borrowing on your future in order to pay for your child's future. After all that information we had earlier in this book about investments for retirement, why would you want to take one of your greatest investments and leverage it for college expenses? Yet millions of parents make that devastating financial choice every year. I'm talking about avoiding any college funding plan that includes a home equity loan or home equity line of credit or refinancing an existing home mortgage. These options reduce the amount of equity in your home, increasing the risk of possible foreclosure, and you incur costs in interest charges that may cost you more if the term on the new mortgage is greater than the remaining term of the existing mortgage. For example, if there are ten years left on the mortgage, and parents get a new thirty-year loan, then they will have to make mortgage payments for another twenty years. Furthermore, if parents choose to pull out enough money in equity for four years of college all at once, then they will pay interest on money that won't yet be needed until the upcoming sophomore, junior, and senior years.

Ask the Right Question

When I was a young adult, got married, and began having kids (in that order), I was first exposed to the whole idea of "the college my child gets accepted into." As a mom of many who has already launched a few college-bound kiddos, I'm still hearing, "What college did they get accepted into?" The part of that question that amazes me is that the answer that is most impressive is also the most expensive (Columbia, Harvard, Stanford, Yale). These schools have average four-year costs for tuition and room and board of $206,000 (Columbia), $195,000 (Harvard and Stanford), and $193,000 (Yale). While an average of 40 percent of the students who attend these high-cost institutions of higher learning receive financial aid, grants, or scholarships, the money only averages out to about $9,300 of assistance per year.[2] This leaves a boatload of money that the student and Mom and Dad owe for college. Most of this is usually found in loans of some kind. And this means that the average graduates from the most prestigious colleges have student loans upward of $100,000.

So why is the question, "What college did they get accepted into?"

The question should be, "What college did they get accepted into that *we can afford*?"

Why do you want to leverage your future (through home equity loans and lines of credit or other loans) or hinder their future (through massive student-loan debt) when it will take many years of earning power for them to pay back those loans? One of the most common problems I hear about has to do with the burden of dual student loans in a young marriage.

The new mantra should be, I will go to the school where I can get the best education possible for the least amount of student-loan debt.

One of the best things you can do for your college fund is teach your kids a good work ethic at home and school. Ride the homework train on them in the afternoons. Teach them that getting good grades, pursuing passions in sports, academics, and the arts, and working hard are their main jobs in high school. And be sure to let them know you expect them not only to get scholarships but to participate in work-study programs, have jobs in the summer and between college semesters, and earn part of their way through school. The sooner they realize this, the better off everyone will be.

Invest in Creative Savings Methods

Before we discuss traditional financial savings plans to pay for college, let's consider the fact that any way you pay for college that does not involve a cash investment is more money in the bank for you and your student. The ideas listed in this chapter are ways to pay for a college degree through plans that are available for those who are forward thinking and purposeful in their desire to provide a debt-free college experience. We've used several of these for our kids, and every $1,000 that you don't have to spend on tuition, college credit, books, and room and board is $1,000 that will counter the huge student-loan debt that most parents assume as par for the education course. It's an adage I've used before in this book: a penny saved is *more* than a penny earned, especially when it comes to paying for college!

Giving Matters!

Giving involves more than just money; it can include time and talents as well. Here is where some of that giving pays off for college. When you've trained your child to give back to the community, don't let those good deeds go unrewarded. Organizations such as Teach for America (www.teachforamerica.org), the Peace Corps (www.peacecorps.gov), and AmeriCorps (www.americorps.org) all offer educational service awards to students seeking cash and a way to make a difference in the world. The best part is that, unlike other scholarships and grants, these service awards won't affect any federal financial aid eligibility. Even if your student has already acquired student loans, organizations including the Army National Guard, National Health Service Corps, and the National Institutes of Health all sponsor loan-forgiveness programs that turn borrowed cash into free dough in exchange for postgraduate service.

Free Money!

Any time you can get free money for college, it makes sense to do so. By going to www.upromise.com and signing up for a free membership, you can shop at restaurants, stores, gas stations, and even Realtors and have a percentage deposited into a 529 plan account for your child. The good news is that grandparents, friends, and others can sign up and help you too. Some of the families I've interviewed have saved $5,000 or more by subscribing to this source of free money!

Double Dipping: College Credit in High School

Check out these options for your high school children.

Advanced Placement and International Baccalaureate. Several of our kids have taken Advanced Placement (AP) or International Baccalaureate (IB) classes throughout their high school years. These are college-level courses that are offered at their high school. At the end of the year, they take a test to see if they score high enough to get college credit. The cost of the test is more than offset by the value of the college credit that will be awarded to your students if they pass. It is important to note that not all colleges accept these credits, so it will be important to check with the admissions office of the college of your choice. A secondary benefit of these courses is that they can help students get into college, because having AP and IB credit makes for very good résumé fodder in college applications. It shows ambition and a good school\work ethic. For information regarding your state's programs, go to the National Association for College Admission Counseling (www.nacacnet.org).

Dual enrollment classes. One of the coolest ways to pay for college is to let your local high school district help pay for it while your child is still in high school. Many school districts now partner with local colleges to offer college credit for high school students who take classes at a nearby community college. Consequently, these classes count toward both high school and college degree requirements. There are thousands of kids each year who graduate from high school one day and then receive an associate's degree the next day.

Be aware that these programs vary from district to district and state to state. In some cases, the dual enrollment classes take place in the high school during the regular school day. Yet other programs require students to attend classes on the college campus, alongside other college students. The average college savings for a two-year associate's degree at state tuition rates is $3,200.

Balance in all things. Bob and I are careful about the fact that we want our kids to be kids and not have adult responsibilities too soon. There is, however, a balance. While we are real sticklers on homework and housework and don't allow the kids to treat us like we're maids, we do understand that they are still kids and need to have fun in their childhood. Consequently, if they are enrolled in AP, IB, or college classes while in high school, we try to make sure that they do not overdo it. We limit their extracurricular activities and discourage a regular part-time job so that their primary job will be to get good grades in their advanced courses. It would be a self-defeating effort to have them take advanced or college classes only to have their overly busy schedules negate their ability to get good grades. Remember, there is no credit if they don't pass the AP or IB tests or pass the college course they are taking! So look closely at the curriculum before you sign up your student for these classes, establish work-study habits, set boundaries to preserve the integrity of their grades, and leave room for kids to be kids and have fun!

Community First, Four-Year Later

I was talking to a professor with a PhD at a nearby university. She was well respected in the academic community and had a rewarding career in her field. She started off at junior college. Her dad sat her down when she was in high school and said, "Never pay more than you have to pay for anything. You don't need to attend all four years at a major university. You can go to junior college and then transfer, and you will save more than $30,000 in tuition." This is what she did, and she never regretted it. She was able to graduate without a massive debt load. (I've talked to some who graduated with more than $100,000 in student loans and will spend the next twenty years paying them off!)

Think of it as a half-price sale for education: you buy two years at full price, then get two for half off or more. The average community college tuition rate is 40 percent of the average tuition rate at four-year public colleges and 10 percent of the average tuition rate at four-year private institutions. If your children attend a community college for two years, you'll not only save money on tuition, you'll also save on room, board, and transportation by having them stick close to home. The key to getting the most value for your education dollar is to make sure these college credits are transferable and be assured that they are working toward the four-year college goal.

Employee Discount

My high school friend Karyn Maxwell had a dad who was a baseball coach. He worked his way up to the college level, and by the time Karyn's older sister graduated from high school, he was the baseball coach at Texas Christian University. Both Karyn and her sister went there for free because of his employee benefits. If you or your child have some latitude in your career, consider working at a local college for the tuition benefits it can afford you or your child.

Most universities offer some form of tuition remission to their full-time employees, and others extend the benefit to part-time employees as well. If you want to go this route, be sure you know the vesting process, because sometimes you have to be working there for a certain number of years before your children and spouse will qualify for free tuition. If you can't secure a staff position at the school of your choice, don't forget that many companies offer tuition reimbursement packages. A study conducted by the Society for Human Resource Management estimates that 67 percent of all employers offer financial assistance to employees seeking an undergraduate degree.[3]

Scholarships

Millions of dollars in scholarship money goes unclaimed every year. This is free lunch money that parents or prospective students who are willing to do some detective work may find more quickly than they think. For instance, www.salliemae.com has more than 1.9 million scholarships valued at 16 billion dollars to research! Your child, for example, could write a five-hundred-word essay on skateboarding, get rewarded for being a bowler, or have his interest in hunting redeemed with a nice scholarship. Or you can find many other areas of interest, because there are thousands of scholarships that go unused every year because kids don't apply for them.

Early is better than later. Some scholarships are only available to high school juniors. Other military academy scholarships require academic, athletic, and community excellence starting from the freshman year in high school. Don't forget to have students apply to local civic organizations and community scholarships as well. Your high school counselor should have a list of these scholarships.

✓ *The 60-Minute College Plan Workout Tip Sheet*

1. Make-Up-Your-Mind Warmup (5 minutes)
- Say something positive about the results of the pretest to your spouse and college-bound student.
- Decide on the topic you will cover for this workout.
- Commit to having a successful hour.

2. Strength Training (10 minutes)
- Write down the results of the pretest that reveal areas of weakness.
- List the means of overcoming obstacles indicated on the pretest.

3. Cardio Burn (20 minutes)
- Read out loud to your spouse and child the detailed notes in the section "First Things First" and then your chosen section.
- Gather research information and fully familiarize yourself with the topic.
- Put written notes and other research information you've printed into the pocket folder for this chapter.

4. Take Your Heart Rate (20 minutes)
- Take action for your topic.
- Keep copies of any documentation, scholarship applications, etc.
- Delegate responsibilities for this topic.

5. *Congratulations Cool Down (5 minutes)*

- Say something positive about your progress today and/or your spouse and college-age child.
- Set the topic and time for your next workout.

The 60-Minute Passion for a Home-Based Business Workout

Twelve years ago my first book, *Shop, Save, and Share,* was published. Close to the time I was starting a new career, one of my best friends, Brenda Taylor, launched her home-based business as a jeweler for Premier Designs. We were both able to grow these home-based businesses and find success in our respective fields.

I loved money matters and helping people to navigate their financial problems. I enjoyed speaking before audiences. I was in the zone in interviews on television and radio. I thoroughly appreciated having books in print. (Note: I did not say I liked *writing* the books!) Few writers are able to make their living by writing—most are part time or waiting for a big break.

Brenda is an intelligent woman who attended Auburn University and graduated from the Mississippi University for Women. She's also as southern as they come, from her graciously written thank-you notes, to her perfectly coiffed hair, to the aristocratic way she enters a room—poised and confident. Think Sandra Bullock in the movie *The Blind Side,* only a tall, lovely brunette instead of a blonde. As a self-respecting belle, Brenda sees value in a highly accessorized life. She loves jewelry, is very stylish, and is gifted at putting together an impressive ensemble. By parlaying that passion into a productive business, she's become a diamond designer in the company, which is helping her family live in financial freedom and also helping to put their kids through college.

The main reason for both her success and mine is one word: *passion*.

The fun thing about living a parallel life in business with my girlfriend is that we enjoy talking about our businesses to each other even though we are in radically different businesses. There are a lot of places our respective fields overlap. It's always fun to broaden your perspective by hearing about someone else's passion. I recently discovered that, because of my friend's passion, I know more about the Premier Designs company than some of their jewelers.

The following workout will help you not only discover what gets you up in the morning, but how that passion can be leveraged into a profitable home-based business. In fact, 45 percent of all businesses owned by women are based at home.[1] It's really okay if some of these passions and interests end up making money for the family coffers. In fact, that's kind of the point!

Preworkout Test

For this test, look for the section in this chapter called "Primary Areas of Interest" and then do the following:

1. Go through this list and put a check by the areas that moderately interest you.

2. Go through the list a second time and look at the checked items, then put a second check by the areas that interest you the most.

3. Now, forget about the list and think about other passion areas that may not be listed but that would also be of great interest to you. Write those down on a sheet of paper to be used during the workout.

The majority of home-based businesses fail within the first two years.[2] You can think of examples of this from your circle of friends and family. Take a second to think about the different home-based businesses they've launched and how successful they were. Maybe they started selling Mary Kay and ended up giving it away for half price at a garage sale. It might have been a cake business that ended up yielding the baker only a buck a cake. You might be your own best example from businesses you've had in the past that failed to make money or even cost you money. While passion is the key, practicality comes in a close second in terms of the necessities for success in business. If you can't make money, then it's just a nice hobby and not a business.

This workout will marry your passion (type of business based on interest) to the practical (kind of business based on that section in the information that will follow). This workout is only designed to help you do the appropriate research and narrow your search so that you can discover what type and kind of business is most likely to succeed with your money personality.

Don't have any further expectations than those first two. The next step will come in the following chapter when you are ready to launch a business. By taking two hours (this workout and the next chapter's), you can save thousands of dollars and thousands of hours on a business that would otherwise fail. These workouts are going to set you up for success!

The 60-Minute Passion for a Home-Based Business Workout

1. Make-Up-Your-Mind Warmup (5 minutes)

Say something positive about your passion and how you are good at it. Take a minute or two to dream about what it would be like to make your passion profitable in a satisfying home-based business. Commit to finding the type and kind of home-based business that best fits your passion and skills.

2. Strength Training (10 minutes)

Write down the results of the pretest, listing the items checked once and twice plus any areas of interest you added to the list. This is going to be the *type of business* you will enter based on your passion and areas of interest. You will be matching these up with *kinds of business,* and then in the next chapter, you'll finish the workout that will help you launch your business.

List the means of overcoming obstacles you see that might prevent you from discovering your passion. If you have had a business in the past, write down why the business was successful or why it was not. These are also obstacles you must overcome, especially if you've launched the wrong type or kind of business in the past. Keep all these records in your pocket folder for home-based business workouts.

3. Cardio Burn (20 minutes)

Read the detailed notes in the sections "Pursuing Your Passion Through Research and Analysis" and "Kinds of Businesses." If you are working out with a spouse, family member, or other potential business partner, read this out loud for understanding. Determine what research you still need to do from the material in this section, such as more library searches or Internet searches. Determine what kind of business will work best for your personality and skill set and visit the Small Business Administration Web site (www.sba.gov) to find out how you can take the personality and skills assessment test.

4. Take Your Heart Rate (20 minutes)

Any research you have not done can be done during this time. Delegate responsibilities to other participants in this workout with a specific due date so that the next time you do this workout, you'll have the information on hand that you need to complete this project. Do not make a decision on which home-based business to launch during this workout. Keep an open mind. Decide the type of business (based on your passion and area of interest) and the kind of business (based on the material in this chapter and your own research) that will work best for you. Write these down and put them in the pocket file folder for this workout.

5. Congratulations Cool Down (5 minutes)

Say something positive about your progress today to yourself, your spouse, family member, and/or potential business partner. Set the time and topic for your next workout.

Pursuing Your Passion Through Research and Analysis

One of the best ways to start looking at a home-based business is to do a lot of research:

- Ask your librarian to help research your chosen field.
- Look up books, magazines, and newspaper articles.
- Talk to other people who have done what you'd like to do.
- Join an industry organization.
- Subscribe to industry publications that are related to your area of interest.

The first part of research is to determine your passions and interests. A big part of the success of your business is also dependent upon knowing your money personality, so if you have not yet done "The 60-Minute (Split) Personality Workout," I suggest you do that first. It's important to take a personal skills and interest inventory, which is what we are going to do in this section.

If you want to take such research a bit further, you can get a free assessment called "Personality I.D.," which is a new, unique, and valid interactive personality assessment tool that allows the respondent to view himself or herself and others from a fresh, new perspective. Its primary purpose is to help an individual identify and understand his or her unique personality as it relates to business. By understanding your personality and how it causes you to operate, it might be easier to decide what kind of home business would best suit you. Find Personality I.D. at www.careerdirect online.org or www.crown.org/tools/personality.aspx. These assessments may also be available at a local library, community center, college, or from the Small Business Administration (www.sba.gov).

With imagination and talent, a hobby can become a source of income. Here are some primary areas of interest that are most common among the stay-at-home moms (SAHMs) I surveyed, as well as the businesses that have emerged from such interests.

Primary Areas of Interest
Animals
> pet grooming
> animal breeding
> pet sitting/walking
> cleaning pet yards
> pet taxi service

Antiquing
> refurbishing and resale
> acquisition and resale
> consignment sales
> eBay sales
> bird-dog shopper for antique stores

Art
> interior design
> room/wall murals
> painting sales/consignment
> furniture manufacturing (specialty design)
> manufacturing
> gallery shows

Bargain Hunting
    writing/topical articles/book sales
    eBay sales business
    consignment sales
    perpetual garage sales/flea market sales

Cooking
    cake decorating/sales
    candy making
    catering
    caterer subcontractor (only provides desserts or other specialty product)
    meals-to-go for busy moms
    cookie sales (Guess where Mrs. Field's cookies started?)
    cookbook author
    specialty condiments
    bed-and-breakfast cooking
    menu planning

Children
    child care services
    children's party planner
    children's party bags
    tutoring
    preschool day trip provider
    munchkin minder

Computers
    Web site design
    Web site maintenance
    newsletter management
    desktop publishing

legal transcriptionist
direct mail provider
personal organizer
travel planning
mail-order sales
online auctions
troubleshooting and repair
virtual assistant

Crafting

manufacturing and sales
consignment sales
lamps and lampshades specialties
craft fairs
interior design
scrapbooking provider
flea market sales
children's parties
school "craft day" provider
card making

Electronics

media services
video/DVD demo services
electronic repairs

Entertaining

bed-and-breakfast
catering
party planner
party consultant

Finances

> virtual assistant
> daily money management
> personal money management
> seniors money management assistance
> budget consultant
> seminars on money management

Music

> private home instruction
> tutoring
> customized music videos
> special events coordinator/consultant
> reviewer

People

> party planner
> consultant
> personal profile writer
> freelance media relations
> phone pollster
> home-based sales
> errand service

Photography

> desktop media design
> sales (home studio or on location)
> brochures and trifolds
> video demo reels
> display design
> consignment

photography instructor
photography writer

Physical Fitness

personal trainer
massage therapy
instructor
children's activity coordinator
consultant
fitness writer

Reading

online book sales and resale (eBay and Amazon)
editing
writing
reviewer
researcher
consultant
tutoring

Selling

eBay and Internet sales
multilevel marketing sales
mail-order sales
network marketing
phone sales
catalog sales

Shopping/Buying

personal shopper
buy and sell (consignment or Internet)

grocery personal shopper
virtual assistant

Scrapbooking

design
scrapbook services
scrapbook material sales
in-home classes

Sewing

alterations
repairs
custom sewing
costumes
design
instruction
interior design

Speaking

public speaking
women's conferences
speaking coach
instruction
consulting
seminars

Teaching

tutoring
home class instruction
education consultant
education writer

Tutoring
    math
    reading
    music
    English
    language
    science

Writing
    newspaper freelancer
    magazine articles
    church or school newsletters
    books
    editor
    desktop publishing
    Web site content
    writers' conference faculty
    online writer

Kinds of Businesses
The next action is to understand the different kinds of businesses and their classifications.

Service Business
This is the easiest kind of business to set up and usually requires the smallest initial investment and the simplest bookkeeping. It also tends to be an easy business to run from home. A service business may also require some experience and is more likely to be subject to state licenses and regulations. If you do something well—fixing things, painting or decorating, writing or editing, cutting hair, fixing or programming computers—these are but a few possibilities for your own service business. And if you are

good at something, you might consider teaching those skills to others. Be imaginative. Don't ignore your own resources.

Sales Business

Sales can take many different forms, from retail or wholesale to storefront, mail order, direct sales, or network marketing. There are also consignment sales and Internet sales as well. Bookkeeping tends to be a little more complex, depending upon the kind of sales you offer. There tends to be more flexibility (including hours of operation) in a sales business as opposed to a service business. In sales, whenever interests change, the sales business can change with them.

There might be a need to carry inventory, which could be a start-up cost to consider for supplies and materials. Tax laws, credit card services, and banking issues are more complicated in a sales-based business.

Manufacturing

For the majority of home-based businesses, this means crafts of some kind: jewelry, leather, clothing, pottery, furniture, home décor, etc. Crafts offer an opportunity for a craftsperson to do what she enjoys for pleasure and to get paid for it as well. The key in manufacturing as a business is to offer a product that others also enjoy. An awful-looking necklace made of acorns may have been fulfilling to make, but if no one buys it, then you don't have a business.

Virtual Work

This is home-based work performed online where you work on a contract or "for hire" basis. In some of these businesses, you do not have benefits and will receive a 1099 form. You will still file an IRS Schedule C on your taxes as a home-based business. The keys to this kind of business are:

Maximizing your résumé for virtual work employers. Quite a few work-at-home job seekers make the mistake of using a regular employment kind of résumé to get a virtual job. This only tells the potential employer that you are not familiar with remote work experiences. Be sure to highlight your ability to work independently as well as your familiarity with online collaboration tools and other communication options.

Good research skills. Predators abound in this kind of business, and you can easily be taken advantage of if you haven't done your research on virtual work. The key lies in using good versus bad search terms when looking for this kind of work. For sixty of the best search terms, go to www.ratracerebellion.com/google_search.html (or visit the home page at www.ratracerebellion.com). You will need to learn to spot the scams with red flags such as exaggerated income claims, photos of luxury mansions and cars, and any ongoing credit charges in the fine print. If you have to submit your credit card information to get a job, then it's likely a scam. You can also validate a company's legitimacy by checking its status at the Better Business Bureau (www.bbb.org).

Ongoing courses. Take courses online or at your local community college to keep your skills polished and up-to-date. You can find free or low-cost certifications at sites such as www.brainbench.com. These will make you more competitive for virtual work.

☑ The 60-Minute Passion for a Home-Based Business Workout Tip Sheet

1. Make-Up-Your-Mind Warmup (5 minutes)
- Say something positive about your passion and how you are good at it.
- Commit to finding the home-based business that best fits your passion and skills.

2. Strength Training (10 minutes)
- Write out the results of the pretest, listing the items checked once and twice as well as your write-in areas of interest.
- List a means of overcoming obstacles that might prevent you from discovering your passion.

3. Cardio Burn (20 minutes)
- Read the detailed notes under the "Pursuing Your Passion Through Research and Analysis" and "Kinds of Businesses" sections.
- Determine what research you still need to do from the material in this section.
- Determine which kind of business will work best for your personality and skill set.

4. Take Your Heart Rate (20 minutes)
- Continue any research you have not done.
- Do *not* make a decision on which home-based business to launch during this workout.

- Decide what type of business (based on your passion and area of interest) and what kind of business (based on the material in this chapter and your own research) will work best for you.

5. Congratulations Cool Down (5 minutes)
- Say something positive about your progress today and/or about your spouse.
- Set the time and topic for your next workout.

The 60-Minute Launch Your Home-Based Business Workout

Nearly 600,000 businesses opened this year, and by the year after next, according to the Small Business Administration, only half of those will still be in existence.[1] The numbers are even higher for home-based businesses. This, however, doesn't mean that all these businesses fail, it just means that only half of them stick around. If you are going to work for another company in a direct sales type of venture, then all companies are not created equal. It's been my observation that one of the main reasons people lose money on a home-based direct sales venture is because they have to put the up-front costs on a credit card, and then they discover halfway through the year that they aren't cut out to sell. By then, though, the investment and commitment have already been made, and they find that they've worked a year for free just to fulfill the commitment they didn't fully consider or research.

This workout is essential before you decide which business to launch. By the time you're done with this critical hour, you will have a clear business plan and be ready to launch a successful home-based business.

Preworkout Test

To be prepared for this workout, it's important to read the following six steps and answer any questions that arise.

Step 1: Can You Hack It?

The most necessary skill is the ability to show up. But don't confuse passion with talent—both are needed to start a legitimate home-based business. Also needed are the abilities to handle bookkeeping, time management, marketing, etc.

Isolation and rejection are often early-business companions. Successful entrepreneurs will need to be able to take these undesirable partners by the hand and learn how to walk alongside them for a season. A client hates the way the designed scrapbook turned out. The cake wasn't the right flavor. The desktop project took so much time that the profit was little more than fifty cents an hour. All of these are par for the course when it comes to establishing a home business. Home-based business owners need to consider seriously whether this is a good choice for their personality and their family.

Step 2: Focus on What People Need

Successful small business owners often target what people need, and it just so happens that these needs reflect a present or former need that the home-based business owners had at one time as well. That was certainly my case. My family had a financial need, and I wanted to help meet that need and stay at home with our babies. That's why I feel that the most successful home-based businesses are those that incorporate the entire family—and if the kids don't work in the business, then they are at least supportive of it and understand why Mom and/or Dad is doing this.

When I first started "Shop, Save, and Share Seminars," it was a tiny operation that made no profit for three years. It targeted a financial need among stay-at-home moms and those trying to get out of debt. Our kids were two, four, six, eight, and ten years old at the time. That operation has grown up into Ellie Kay and Company, LLC, and is making profits to benefit the Kay Education Fund (smile intended) as well as several legitimate nonprofit organizations.

There's a team that works hard for me, and it includes a literary agent, a spokesperson agent, a publicist, an office assistant, a stylist, and a professional cleaner.

Among my other employees are the "Kay Kids," who perform the following duties: direct mail services, Internet sales, PowerPoint design, media relations, CD duplication, media kit marketing, on-site sales, postal metering, public relations coordination, and anything else I can think up to keep them gainfully employed and feeling like a part of the business team.

My point is that, in my case, I started teaching a few coupon seminars because I had a business background (as a broker), enjoyed public speaking, and wanted to help other moms learn how to stretch their food dollars. This cottage industry has always been home-centered, and it grew to the point that it will hopefully fund all five of the children's college education while teaching them a work ethic and providing a valuable service to the community.

Step 3: Test the Business Idea First

Your mom may love your chocolate truffles, but it doesn't mean that you can sell enough of them to qualify as a home business. It might cost more, in terms of time and supplies, than it is worth. It's critical for future small business owners to test their ideas among a sample market. One way to test the market is to get last year's phone book. Go through the yellow pages and call similar businesses to see if they are still in operation. This gives you an idea of whether the goods or services are viable for your community. Invest the time and energy in research. Go to the Small Business Administration's (SBA) resource partner, the Service Corps of Retired Executives, for more research, as well as help from local business development centers and networking groups. For example, if you decide you want to launch a freelance writing career, it would be a good idea to attend a local writers' workshop or writers' group to see how many others are turning a profit and how they are making it work.

Step 4: Stay in Touch with Trends

Party planners need to know what kids like. Photographers need to have an eye for what the marketplace wants. Personal shoppers need a constant fashion update to remain viable. Keep in mind that millennials want a scaled-down version for their kids of what is popular among adults. Women in their fifties want style that is new and fresh while keeping with their lifestyle. Editors want writers who know what readers are demanding. Desktop publishing clients want materials that are cutting edge. A virtual personal assistant was unheard of a decade ago. Now, busy working moms and corporate execs want someone to see that the household bills are paid and the gardener gets his paycheck. By keeping up with trends, your new business can capitalize on the needs in the marketplace and provide you and your family with a maximum return for a minimum time investment.

Step 5: Consider Servicing Established Businesses

During times of layoffs, often the first people let go are those who provide peripheral services, such as information technology departments, benefits departments, and even human resources. Many of these can be outsourced to independent contractors. Some companies hire consultants (that is, employees without benefits) to replace them, and often these consultants work from home. With the right job skills and an eye toward market trends, savvy small business owners can service those companies.

Step 6: The Family Council

Once a small business owner has gathered enough information, it's time to have a family sixty-minute workout. The first workout should be with your spouse, and then you should work out with your family. If you are reading this information for the pretest, then this is something you can come back to and do with the entire family at a later date. During this meeting, it's important to discuss all sides of the issue. Sometimes a husband might see certain advantages and disadvantages that his wife may not see, and at other times a man's understanding is limited until he sees his wife's perspective. Start by considering three different kinds of home businesses, and discuss the pros and cons of each, including start-up costs, a realistic time commitment, and the projected net income (gross income minus your costs).

The 60-Minute Launch Your Home-Based Business Workout

This workout is best completed with everyone who will be involved in the launch and daily operation of your home-based business. This may be a spouse or family member, but it might also include a business professional who may be sponsoring you if you are involved in direct sales or services. At the bare minimum, this professional should be able to answer the questions about the business (number of shows required, total initial investment amount, etc.). If he or she is not willing to answer these questions, that is a red flag. But if she or he tries and does not have all the answers, then that is okay. Just have them answer as many as they know. If you are looking at more than one direct sales company, then your sponsoring professional's answers will give you a better basis for a comparison in making your decision between the candidates.

1. Make-Up-Your-Mind Warmup (5 minutes)
Say something positive about your desire to launch your own business. Commit to working through this entire chapter and workout. Decide that

if you don't get through all the material this time, it's all right and you were still successful. Making progress is what is important.

2. Strength Training (10 minutes)

Write down your impressions as a result of reading the six steps on the pretest. The pretest can actually be a sixty-minute workout if you desire, otherwise it's a plumb line to make sure that the walls of protection around your decision are straight and solid.

List the means of overcoming obstacles as indicated on the pretest steps. If you are not willing to work through the points brought up in the pretest steps, then do not continue this workout.

3. Cardio Burn (20 minutes)

Read the detailed notes from this chapter for understanding. If you are reading with a spouse, family member, or other potential business partner, read this out loud while the other takes notes as recommended. Take notes about the research you need to do, points that need further clarification, or specific items that would apply to your business. You will need to fill out the chart in the next block of time, so make notes that can help toward that end as you read through the material. Keep materials in a pocket folder labeled "Home-Based Business."

4. Take Your Heart Rate (20 minutes)

This part of the workout will take some time. If you don't have all the information at hand, then fill out what you can on the detailed "Home-Based Business Plan Chart" on page 185 and write down what information you still need so you can research it. Once you've completed this workout (and it may take more than one hour to complete), you are finally in a position to launch your home-based business. It's a good idea to periodically repeat this workout to make sure that your business is on track and to add any ideas on how to keep it fresh and growing to take it to the next level of success.

5. Congratulations Cool Down (5 minutes)

Say something positive about your progress today to yourself, your spouse, a family member, or your potential business partner. Set the time and topic for your next workout.

Home-Based Business Information

Independent versus Interdependent Businesses

Home-based businesses have something in common: they are all owned by independent small business owners. This chapter will only address sole proprietorship businesses (one owner), not partnerships or corporations. Many sole proprietorship businesses are independent contractors who file their own taxes but have another employer. Examples include a direct sales company (DSC) or multilevel marketing (MLM) associate.

There's a huge difference between manufacturing jewelry independently versus signing on as a jeweler with a company like Premier Designs. This next section will help determine the difference between coming in under another business as an independent contractor and forging a brand-new business by yourself.

Direct Selling Companies

When it comes to selling a product or service under another company while retaining a sole proprietorship status, it's more important than ever to do some market research. These companies identify themselves with different terms; some are also called multilevel marketing (MLM) or direct sales (DSC). Many of these offer products (such as bakeware, toys, or jewelry) and are sold through home parties. Consultants can recruit other consultants for the company and gain a portion of their profits as well. This usually holds true for three levels of consultants. Thus it is sometimes referred to as tri-level marketing.

Here are a few items to research when choosing to represent a DSC and the questions that need answers in order for you to make a good decision:

- What are the up-front start-up costs (application fees, joining fees, authorization fees, etc.)?
- What kind of a down payment is required?
- What are the average gross profits for consultants?
- What is the hostess plan like (free merchandise, bonus incentives, etc.)?
- What are the customer shipping and handling fees?
- How will you be considered for promotion in leadership to the next level?
- What are the benefits of leadership at the next levels?
- What percentage of retail does the consultant make?
- What percentage of generations or down lines (people the consultant recruits to work for the DSC) do the consultants get?
- How many down line generations are paid?
- Do you have to sign up a certain number of down line consultants before you get a percentage?
- Does the DSC print, track, and report down line activity, or is it up to the consultant to get this information directly?
- Can down line members break away or get promoted from under you?
- Do you have to cover specific territories?
- Are you required to fill out sales reports or call-ins?
- How much inventory is needed?
- How much does the inventory cost to start the business?
- What are the required minimum monthly or annual sales?
- Does the DSC have corporate debt or does it operate debt free?
- Is the DSC listed with the Better Business Bureau? (Conduct your own search at www.bbb.org.)

- Is the DSC a member of the Direct Selling Association (DSA)? (Conduct your own search at www.dsa.org.)
- Do consultants have to package and ship orders or does the DSC handle this?
- How many home shows are required each month? Is there a minimum requirement?
- Are you paid up-front?
- Do consultants have to handle state sales tax issues or does the DSC?

Bonus Information for Future Workouts

Tax Tips for the Grown-Up Home-Based Business

SEP: Once a home business starts making money, it's time to consider setting up a simplified employee pension (SEP) in which business owners can contribute up to 25 percent of their compensation (business profits minus the second self-employment tax deduction). I set up a SEP without a certified public accountant's help. It was that easy. There were no IRS forms to file or administration fees to set it up. But my CPA tells me how much to fund it with each year when he prepares my taxes. If you're a sole proprietor, this is a good move since you only file this on yourself, and it will give you a portable retirement fund that you control.

LLC: A decision to put your sole proprietorship under the structure of a limited liability company is under the growing-up phase of your business. LLCs are not as tightly regulated as limited partnerships, and they offer greater liability protection. In researching the next step or growing-up step in my business—defining it as an LLC, S Corp, limited liability partnership (LLP), etc.—I found that an LLC offered many of the benefits with few of the drawbacks of other incorporation options. I formed Ellie Kay and Company, LLC, by walking through the process with a business mentor. My CPA was surprised that I was able to do it so easily, but my mentor had already set up four such companies.

Home-Based Business Plan Chart

Type of Business	Pros	Cons	Start-Up Costs	Weekly Time Commitment	Projected Net Income
Business Option 1					
Business Option 2					
Business Option 3					
Business Option 4					

Once again, this is a topic where you do the research for your own small business and trust your CPA or accountant to advise you. Can I add something else about an LLC? Once I did this and put it on all contracts, 1099 forms, stationery, invoices, etc., I found that my credibility level jumped ten rungs. I wasn't perceived as some chickie-poo sorting coupons in her basement. Forming an LLC gave my trademarked brand and business the additional credibility it deserved as I came to be perceived as an author, speaker, spokesperson, and media professional.

Employees: Another significant tax question to put to your accountant has to do with employees. Most of us will have contract labor where we employ independent contractors (who get no benefits) rather than traditional employees (who get Social Security, health insurance benefits, and workers' compensation).

If you pay someone $600 or more, you will need them to sign a W-9 form (download at www.irs.gov) with their information and Social Security or employer identification number (EIN). You will have to file 1099-MISC forms for all your contractors at the end of the year and mail them to the contractors by January 31. Then you'll file a Form 1096 with the IRS. All of this is information your CPA will handle or advise you on.

BIG POINT: Do *not* get into trouble with the IRS by paying an independent contractor $600 or more and then making the mistake of *not* filing a 1099 and 1096. If you pay an editor $600 to review your proposal or a Web site designer $700 to redo your site or a housekeeper $2,000 a year to clean your office or your baby college boy $800 a year to do your PowerPoints, then file the appropriate forms, or you're paying them under the table. If they don't have a Social Security number, don't hire them. Then if you are ever nominated to the Supreme Court, you won't have to worry about investigators finding out that you paid your housekeeper on the sly because she was an illegal immigrant. Be above reproach and have a CPA or your business mentor show you where you're doing something stupid that you didn't know was against the law.

☑ The 60-Minute Launch Your Home-Based Business Workout Tip Sheet

1. Make-Up-Your-Mind Warmup (5 minutes)
- Say something positive about your desire to launch your own business.
- Commit to working through this entire chapter and workout.

2. Strength Training (10 minutes)
- Write down your impressions as a result of reading the six steps on the pretest.
- List the means of overcoming obstacles indicated on the pretest.
- If you are not willing to work through the pretest steps, then do not continue this workout.

3. Cardio Burn (20 minutes)
- Read the detailed notes from this chapter for understanding. Make notes about the research you need to do, points that need further clarification, or specific items that would apply to your business.
- You will need to fill out the chart in the next block of time, so make notes that can help toward that end as you read.

4. Take Your Heart Rate (20 minutes)
- Fill in the detailed "Home-Based Business Plan Chart."

5. Congratulations Cool Down (5 minutes)
- Say something positive about your progress today and/or about your spouse.
- Set the time and topic for your next workout.

The 60-Minute Couple's Workout

Early in our marriage, I learned that men are not just from another planet, they are a different species, or so it seems. This is particularly true when it comes to the way they communicate. Our good friends Pam and Bill Farrel wrote a best-selling book on the topic, *Men Are Like Waffles— Women Are Like Spaghetti*. Here's what they said about how men and women communicate differently:

If she says...	She really means...
We need.	I want.
It's your decision.	The correct decision should be obvious by now.
Do what you want.	You'll pay for this later.
You're so manly.	You need a shave and you sweat a lot.
This kitchen is so inconvenient.	I want a new house.
You have to learn to communicate.	Just agree with me.
I'm sorry.	You'll be sorry.
You're certainly attentive tonight.	Is sex all you ever think about?

If he says...	**What he really means...**
I'm hungry.	I'm hungry.
I'm sleepy.	I'm sleepy.
I'm tired.	I'm tired.
Do you want to go to a movie?	I'd eventually like to have sex with you.
Can I take you out to dinner?	I'd eventually like to have sex with you.
What's wrong? (first time)	I don't see why you're making such a big deal about this.
What's wrong? (second time)	What meaningless, self-inflicted psychological trauma are you going through now?
What's wrong? (third time)	I guess sex tonight is out of the question.[1]

When Bob and I learned how we communicated differently about money topics, we were able to understand each other better and not argue about these issues. The couple's money workout is something we developed early in our marriage, and it helped make the difference for us in how effective we were in trying to really understand the other person. A side benefit was that more fulfilling communication often led to more fulfilling intimacy. (Guy speak: It led to better sex!)

This workout is designed to help you discuss money matters (or any matters for that matter) with the one you love.

Preworkout Quiz

Before we talk about the "60-Minute Couple's Workout," let's play a game like the famous *Newlywed Game* television show. Get twelve pieces of paper or card stock and two big markers. Now get ready to learn some things about your mate.

1. Complete this sentence: When it comes to money, I wish my partner would stop _____ .

    How do you think your spouse answered this question?

    _____

2. If you won $1,000, how would you spend it? _____

    How would your spouse spend it? _____

3. Circle one answer to the following statement: "I would rather have (a) money, (b) beauty, or (c) brains.

    What would your spouse circle _____

As you answer these questions, I think you'll find that you and your spouse are different. You may discover that you didn't know as much about your mate as you thought you knew, and vice versa. But part of any healthy relationship is realizing that we are different and we can give each other permission to have our own thoughts and feelings about financial matters. The goal, whether you are a newlywed or you've been married forever, is to communicate effectively about money, get on the same team, and find financial freedom!

The 60-Minute Couple's Workout

As we prepare for the workout, it's important to establish boundaries and do a little preparation work. We discussed these boundaries in chapter 1, but here are some basics to keep in mind as you set up boundaries and prepare:

- avoid condescension and negativity
- do not interrupt your partner when he or she is talking
- no name-calling
- no throwing food
- no unanswerable questions ("Does this dress make me look fat?")
- start by saying one positive thing to each other
- end by saying one positive thing to each other
- create an environment that encourages comfort and success

Bob and I developed the sixty-minute money workout because we thought that our talks about money would be a lot less painful if they had a clear start and a clear finish. We knew we wouldn't get all our problems solved in just one hour, but we knew we'd make progress if we kept at it.

1. Make-Up-Your-Mind Warmup (5 minutes)

Begin by taking your spouse's hands, looking into his or her eyes, and saying something affirming. Keep in mind that studies indicate that male/female needs are different from what you might want to think. (Men indicate their number-one desire is to be respected; women respond that their number-one need is to feel loved.)[2] So a wife could tell her husband, "I respect your opinion, and I believe we'll work through our money issues." Or a husband could tell his wife, "I love you and I'm committed to talking and not fighting about our finances." If you're really angry at your spouse and can't think of anything positive to say, you can always say something like, "Nice hair" or "Thanks for not eating onions at dinner."

When you read about people who have lost weight and kept it off, most of their stories begin with a watershed moment when they decided they were sick and tired of being out of shape. The same is true with your finances. You need to decide that you are done with this problem and today you will discuss living on a budget, debt, overspending, or living from paycheck to paycheck. This warmup is when you make that commitment to get into good financial shape.

During this time, select your money workout topic (debt, budgeting, vacations, or any of the workouts from this book) and make up your mind about what you want to accomplish.

2. Strength Training (10 minutes)

It usually takes more than one partner to get a couple into financial trouble. Even if one person does most of the spending, the other partner usually tolerates the destructive behavior in some way.

While step one was to start with affirming words and decide on your money topic, this next section is a time to write down your goals on paper so that you will have a tangible and objective standard to work toward. Decide what you want to accomplish during today's workout, how you would like to see the topic resolved in six months, and what the outcome of your goals will be in the long run. This gives both of you a temporary focus (for today), a long-term focus (for the next few months), and a big-world picture (for the long term). Your goals will depend on your topic of the day. For example, if you are discussing a budget, your goals might include (a) setting up a budget that is real and workable, (b) staying on that budget for the next six months to learn how to spend less than what you make, and (c) having a budget become such a habit that it is a financial vehicle that will get your family out of consumer debt, help you pay for your kids' college, and fund your retirement.

3. Cardio Burn (20 minutes)

In this step, you give feet to your goals. If you're setting up a budget, then write down the specifics and course of action for your topic of the day. This may not seem like a lot of time on this section, but realize that you may not get a budget set during the first workout. You can also carry the work in this section over to your next section—if you don't have extra work in the next session. The key is to keep the discussion moving and to work on what you can. Whatever you missed, you can get to it the next time around. If you want to see an online budget tool, go to www.elliekay.com/financial-resource-center.php.

Discuss and work on a plan for your topic of the day. Yes, this and the next section are the hardest two sections, but they are also the fat-burning phase, where you get the most benefit. Write down a step-by-step plan for your topic, make it realistic, and be sure to give and take when it comes to discussing this topic with your mate. In some cases, you may table a particular point and get back to it later, or you may even agree to disagree.

4. Take Your Heart Rate (20 minutes)

This is the point where you do any work that needs to be done after you've written a step-by-step plan from the previous section. For example, if you need to get the facts on your credit and debt information, now is the time to do it. You could get a free copy of your credit report at www.annualcreditreport.com (everyone is entitled to a free annual credit report from each of the three reporting agencies each year). Or if your topic is saving money, you could use this time to set up an automatic allotment (electronic transfer or deposit) from your paycheck or from your checking to your savings account. If your plan of the day is debt reduction, you may decide to cut up all but two or three credit cards and cancel some of your other open credit accounts. (Be sure to cancel the most recent cards first and keep cards that you've had five years or longer in order to keep the longevity part of your FICO score intact.) Don't procrastinate. Do this during this "work" part of the workout. It will help minimize the temptation to procrastinate on the practical aspects of your workout and also keep you on track with your goal for your topic of the day. If there isn't any outside work for you to do during this time, then feel free to expand your discussion from step 3 to reach closure on your topic of the day.

5. Congratulations Cool Down (5 minutes)

Sit back, grab a glass of something cool to drink, and reflect on all you've accomplished in just one hour. You started on a positive note, and you're going to end positive as well. Take this time to tell your partner one thing that you appreciate about today's workout to end the discussion well. For example, you could say, "I noticed you didn't interrupt me when I was talking. Thanks for giving me that respect. I appreciate it," or "When I got upset and started to cry, I appreciate the way you weren't condescending and that you were kind. Thank you."

Keep in mind that, just as you don't get physically buff in just one workout, your finances aren't going to get in shape after this first try either. But after you and your mate have exercised with this money workout a half a dozen times, you'll find yourself stronger, smarter, and more fiscally fit.

✓ The 60-Minute Couple's Workout Tip Sheet

1. Make-Up-Your-Mind Warmup (5 minutes)
- Say something positive to your spouse.
- Decide on the topic for the workout and make a commitment to its success.

2. Strength Training (10 minutes)
- Decide what you want to accomplish during today's workout.
- Discuss how you would like to see the topic resolved in six months.
- Decide what you'd like the outcome to be in the long run.

3. Cardio Burn (20 minutes)
- Write down your course of action for your topic of the day.
- List a step-by-step plan for your topic.
- Discuss obstacles to your goals and how to overcome them.

4. Take Your Heart Rate (20 minutes)
- Do any work that needs to be done after you've written a step-by-step plan from the previous section.

5. Congratulations Cool Down (5 minutes)
- Say something positive to your spouse.
- Set a time and topic for your next workout.

The 60-Minute Giving Guide Workout

I remember the adage of J. Vernon McGee: "The person who said, 'Give until it hurts,' was a very wise person. If it doesn't hurt then it has little meaning for you." I recently received a letter from a good friend who was amazed at the example set by a woman she knew who was borderline homeless. This woman had gone to India as a part of a group to see how women live in that country. She was so touched by their gratitude for the smallest of necessities that she decided to do something about it when she came back to the United States. This woman had a shoeshine business, and even though she was not religious, she decided to give 25 percent of what she earned to others in need. The first week, a man walked by her chair and gave her $100—without getting his shoes shined. The second week, she won at a poker game and gave her primary opponent 10 percent of her earnings. Her adversary was blessed, and she was richer because of her generosity. If a woman who lives one step away from being homeless can give away a quarter of her income and see an immediate benefit, then maybe we can be challenged to give more as well.

Giving is ultimately sacrificing something you have to help someone who has less than you. Few can turn away from the suffering people of Haiti after the horrendous earthquake in January 2010. There was no hesitation for thousands of people to give their time and money to help alleviate the crisis. I am a firm believer in the power of giving. It is the first 10 in the 10/10/80 Rule. Sharing with others is a critical part of any person's money life. In fact, it makes for good money management.

Preworkout Quiz

When I began to hold my things in open palms rather than clenched fists, all kinds of opportunities to be generous presented themselves. Once, I received five free gourmet cookies on an airplane because I was inconvenienced by a delayed flight. I gave three of them to fellow passengers who hadn't had time to get lunch, and, after all, cookies for lunch are better than no lunch at all.

For this quiz, go through this list and place a check next to the things you've given away in the last six months. Go back through the list a second time and put a check by the items you've ever given away in your lifetime. Go back a third time and put a box (that can be checked later) next to the items you plan on giving away in the next six months.

clothing
food
gifts
cars (or gave someone a ride)
the use of your stuff—washer/dryer, a room for the night, your
    lawn mower (Sorry, guys. We'll return it. I promise!), your boat,
    pool, or camper
money
time
creativity
talents
encouraging words
books

furniture

appliances

tools (even your Sears Craftsman tools with a lifetime guarantee!)

flowers

cards

hugs

art

chocolate

Scoring the Quiz

0 checks: Scrooge! You really need to be visited by three ghosts.

1–3 checks: Somewhat generous. At least you aren't a scrooge, and you are somewhat generous. But you can learn to hold some of the uncommon things a little more loosely.

4–5 checks: Generous. According to statistics, the more generous you are, the more likely you've known what it's like to be without. Congratulations on your open-handed lifestyle.

6 or more checks: Supergenerous. People in this category make the best philanthropists and may even have a gift for giving. I've also found that people who give like this often also have an ability to make money. It's almost as if God knew when he created them that they were born to give.

The 60-Minute Giving Guide Workout

I've been able to give from every one of the categories in the pretest, and the results are amazing. There was a time when one of my readers decided to give a school secretary a dozen roses that she had received as a gift. She didn't know how to explain why she did it, just that she needed to do this. The secretary's eyes filled with tears, as she said, "Since my divorce, I never receive flowers. This week was my birthday, and while I got some nice gifts, no one gave me flowers. But when you gave me these, it made me feel like everything will be all right."

This workout helps you decide what organizations mean the most to you personally and where you would like to distribute your giving dollars. If you are a couple, do this exercise individually first and then collectively to decide what to give (not just money), where to give, how much to give, how frequently, and for how long.

1. Make-Up-Your-Mind Warmup (5 minutes)
Say something positive about the results of the pretest. Look at the areas where you've been generous in the recent past and in your lifetime. Think about the way you felt when you opened your hands and let loose of the things you owned. Commit to establishing a workable giving plan.

2. Strength Training (10 minutes)
Write down the results of the pretest, listing the areas where you regularly give, as well as areas where you may be interested in giving. Add to the list things that you've given that weren't included. List the means of overcoming obstacles that keep you from being as generous as you could be.

3. Cardio Burn (20 minutes)
Read the detailed notes on this section. As you read, determine your previous giving pattern and where you could give more. Make a new list of organizations you'd like to further research or places where you and your family could volunteer in the community.

4. Take Your Heart Rate (20 minutes)
Develop a plan on paper to give on multiple levels from multiple categories to multiple groups. Put dates that you will take action by and download forms that will allow you to set up allotments to carry through on

your giving plan. Keep the paperwork from this workout in your pocket folder marked "Giving Workout." Follow through on part of your plan before your next workout.

5. Congratulations Cool Down (5 minutes)
Say something positive about your progress today to yourself, and if you were working in tandem, to your spouse. Set the time and topic for your next workout.

The Sharing Challenge

So how do you learn to be generous when you realize that this is a weak area of your money life? I'm going to suggest some ways you can begin to enjoy the idea of sharing your time, resources, and finances. I challenge you to follow up on one item from this list each week for six weeks. You will find, especially if you haven't yet been very generous, that there is a tremendous feeling of satisfaction that walks alongside generosity. My challenge is simply this: I believe you will feel and live better after you develop the habit of giving. Try it for six weeks, and let me know the results. I look forward to hearing from you.

Simplify!
One of the best ways to help yourself and help others at the same time is to tackle a room, closet, or even a piece of furniture and clean it out. For example, you could choose to start in your bedroom and go through your dresser drawers. Take everything out of each drawer and put it in one of three piles: give away, throw away, and keep. Call a nonprofit organization that needs and wants your donations. Some of them will even come by to pick up your donation. In this cleaning-out process, you are helping to meet the needs of someone else in your community. If you do this with each room in your home, including the garage, not only will you relieve

the clutter, you'll relieve stress in the process of helping others. Does it get any better than that?

Donate

Pay attention to information in your community about specific needs. This information might be found through fliers, in the newspaper, posted on a bulletin board, or in your church's weekly program. Don't ignore these needs. Instead, dedicate fifteen minutes toward collecting specific items that are needed. It might be a matter of donating your soda cans, collecting food items, or gathering specific items of clothing. You might even want to add some of these things to your shopping list and donate new items. If you begin to develop the mind-set of giving, then the next time you hear of a need, you won't be inclined to think, *Oh no! Not again!* Rather, you'll begin to think, *I wonder how I can meet this need in my own way?* You don't have to be extravagant; it really is true that every little bit helps.

Give Time

Our time is one of the most valuable commodities we have today, and it's a great equalizer. Donald Trump has the same twenty-four hours a day as you! Why not look at donating your time to a nonprofit organization? You could plug into a monthly ministry at your church that takes food and clothing to the needy or welcomes new people into the community. You might want to donate a couple of hours a month at a local food pantry or soup kitchen. This could be a great way to spend time with other family members, if you do it together. Our family spends time gathering food and clothing donations for our local homeless shelter, and we deliver them in person. You might get hooked and decide you want to make an even greater time commitment and coach a soccer team, become a Big Sister or Big Brother, or volunteer in a Scouting program. If you're still stumped as to what you can do, visit www.volunteer.com to get more ideas. Giving time would not substitute for donating money to an organization, but it is something almost everyone can give.

Adopt a Third-World Child

When asked why they don't sponsor a child, most families will say they are not certain that their money really goes to that child. You can go to the Better Business Bureau Wise Giving Alliance at www.give.org and request its Wise Giving Guide. This will help you decide which organization to choose. Most sponsorships run anywhere from $25 to $35 per month and provide food, clothing, housing, and education to children. We've had the thrill of watching kids grow up under our sponsorship and go out to become leaders in their communities. Currently, our family sponsors children from three reputable organizations:

World Vision: At World Vision's Web site, click their "Ways to Give" link and choose where you want your dollars to go. World Vision helps children in the United States as well as around the world. Visit www.worldvision.org or call 1-888-511-6548.

Compassion International: This organization is tuned in to crisis and special needs, as well as the general monthly needs of children around the world. It encourages communication with your sponsored child, and you have the chance to see photos and read about how your child is doing in school. It's a great project for your family. Go to www.compassion.com.

Mission of Joy: This is a lesser-known organization that was started by two air force captains when they saw the needs in India. Almost 97 percent of the monthly contributions go directly to India, because the ministry uses volunteer help and has very little overhead. Go to www.missionjoy.org or e-mail the founder at Jeffreyoleary@jeffoleary.com.

Giving Back to Your Community

Your volunteer efforts oftentimes make the difference between allowing a program to continue or letting it fall by the wayside. That translates into areas like your kids getting to compete in soccer games (volunteer coaches), young troops getting cookies at Christmas (annual cookie drives), families being able to buy household goods and clothing at reduced prices (thrift shops), and college scholarships (spouses' organizations). These are only a small sampling of programs that exist because of volunteers. Here are some other ways—and reasons—to get involved.

Meet people: Volunteering alongside others with a like vision forges some of the best and most lasting friendships. Whether it's working with the Red Cross or helping out at a local church, these are great opportunities to meet people.

Support children's activities: Our kids have outside interests, and this sparks a sense of community service within them when they see us volunteering for their groups. Scouting programs, Vacation Bible School, children's unit parties, and sports teams are all ways to keep our kids involved and emotionally, physically, and spiritually healthy.

On-the-job training–enhance résumé: Your volunteer hours in certain areas come with training. Whether it's with the Red Cross at a hospital or at a family support center on computers, you are learning new and marketable skills while gaining valuable experience in a variety of fields. Your volunteer hours and awards on your résumé provide continuity for future employers as you work to help others while building overall experience.

Family project—Operation, Compassionate Kids: Kids can get involved in caring for others around the world. Approach a classroom teacher, Scout leader, or after-school club about sponsoring a different military member each month. In English class, the children can write letters. In art class, they can draw pictures. In Sunday school, they can put together care packages. When a child experiences the blessing of caring in community with others, it can teach lessons in altruism and create an "others" orientation that will last a lifetime. Be sure to get instructions for shipment before sending care packages so that all regulations are followed. Some of the care packages might include:

Toiletries: sample-size shaving cream, disposable razors, wet wipes, deodorant, toothpaste, toothbrush, dental floss, cotton swabs, shampoo, lotion, bug repellent, cool scar (a bandage you put on a scar to help minimize scarring), foot powder, and socks

Food: presweetened drink mix, Slim Jims or jerky, granola bars, energy bars, bag of candy (nonchocolate), gum, canned soup, canned fruit, fruit snacks, nuts, and trail mix

Smart pack: books of all kinds, a modern-translation Bible, crossword puzzles, stationery, stamps, phone cards, online gift certificates, and fact books

Twenty Free Gifts You Can Give

I'd like to end this book with gifts that are of tremendous, even eternal, value that are given at no cost to the giver. These are gifts that any family members can give at any time and in any place. As you seek to live more fiscally responsibly, don't forget to make a difference in the lives of others, and train your children to do the same.

1. Fix broken fences by mending a quarrel.
2. Seek out a friend you haven't seen in a while or who has been forgotten.
3. Hug someone and whisper, "I love you."
4. Forgive an enemy and pray for him.
5. Be patient with an angry person.
6. Express gratitude to someone in your world.
7. Make a child smile.
8. Find the time to keep a promise.
9. Make or bake something for someone else—anonymously.
10. Speak kindly to a stranger and tell her a joke.
11. Enter into another's sorrows and cut the pain in half.
12. Smile. Laugh a little. Laugh a lot.
13. Take a walk with a friend.

14. Kneel down and pat a dog.
15. Lessen your expectations of others.
16. Apologize if you were wrong.
17. Turn off the television and talk.
18. Pray for someone who helped you when you hurt.
19. Give a soft answer even though you feel strongly about that answer.
20. Make friends with someone with whom you have nothing in common—and everything in common.

☑ The 60-Minute Giving Guide Workout Tip Sheet

1. Make-Up-Your-Mind Warmup (5 minutes)
- Say something positive about the results of the pretest.
- Commit to establishing a workable giving plan.

2. Strength Training (10 minutes)
- Write down the results of the pretest.
- List a means of overcoming the obstacles indicated on the pretest that keep you from giving.

3. Cardio Burn (20 minutes)
- Read the detailed notes on this section.
- As you read, determine your previous giving pattern and where you could give more.

4. Take Your Heart Rate (20 minutes)
- Develop a plan on paper to give on multiple levels from multiple categories to multiple groups.
- Keep the paperwork from this workout in your folder labeled "Giving Workout."

5. Congratulations Cool Down (5 minutes)
- Say something positive about your progress today and/or about your spouse.
- Set the time and topic for your next workout.

Acknowledgments

I want to thank my husband, Bob, a.k.a. the World's Greatest Fighter Pilot, for being man enough to let your wife's career path become your ministry. When the chapter of your life that included flying fighters came to an abrupt end, your grace under pressure proved that you are the hero I always knew you were. Thanks go to my precious family—Daniel and Jenn, Philip, Bethany, Jonathan, Joshua, Missy, Moran, Oriah, Eden, and Noia—for their love and support all these years. To those who are related by birth and by marriage, I love you all. There would be no stories, no success, and no book without you.

On a professional level, I have to thank my agent, Steve Laube, who found my first work in the slush pile, guided my career, and eventually landed us with WaterBrook Press. I appreciate your prescient insight in the industry, your ability to navigate everything from writing to speaking and spokesperson work—you never met a contract you couldn't negotiate. Please take your vitamins and get annual checkups, because there are too many people depending on you!

To my publishing friends at WaterBrook: it's a dream come true to be on your team. I have to express my deepest gratitude for your enthusiasm and belief in my work. Thank you, Stephen Cobb, for your leadership and encouragement. Your expertise is priceless. Ken Petersen, thank you for all you've done in publishing in your career. My being a tiny part of your galaxy of publishing stars is such an honor. A special thanks goes to Carie Freimuth for your special effort in marketing, as well as to Tiffany Lauer Walker and Lori Addicott. Special thanks to Pamela Shoup, the production editor who guided this book through proofreading, design, and typesetting—you are so thorough and helpful and I appreciate you! I also want to thank Ginger Kolbaba, my editor, who has been so instrumental in helping me get my message out to you all.

Thanks also to the dear friends who are there in season and out of season—you know who you are, and I'm constantly grateful for your support.

Chapter 5: The 60-Minute Debt Workout

1. Charles R. Swindoll, *The Tale of the Tardy Oxcart* (Nashville: Word, 1998), 38.

2. Credit Advisors Foundation, "Thinking of an Equity Loan?" *Defeat Debt,* August 1999, www.creditadvisors.com/defeat_debt/1999/08/.

3. Mark Solheim, "ABCs of a Great Car Loan," Yahoo! Autos, June 2009, http://autos.yahoo.com/car-finance/basics/us-autos.kiplinger.com/abcs-of-a-great-car-loan.

4. "IRS Urges Taxpayers to e-file Extension Requests by April 15 Filing Deadline," April 2009, www.irs.gov/irs/article/0,,id=206233,00.html.

Chapter 6: The 60-Minute Cha Ching Guide to Paying Less Workout

1. Lucy Lazarony, "Know the Deal on Auto Depreciation," December 26, 2002, www.bankrate.com/brm/news/auto/20011226a.asp.

2. www.theautochannel.com/news/2010/06/07/481580.html

3. Bureau of Labor Statistics, U.S. Department of Labor, "Productivity and Costs, Third Quarter 2009, Preliminary," News Release, November 5, 2009, USDL-09-1330, www.bls.gov/news.release/archives/prod2_11052009.pdf.

4. www.energystar.gov/index.cfm?fuseaction=find_a_product.showProductGroup&pgw_code=LB

Chapter 7: The 60-Minute Travel and Fun Guide Workout

1. "Family Camping Molds Values and an Appreciation for Nature," About.com: Camping, http://camping.about.com/library/weekly/aa020501a.htm.

Chapter 10: The 60-Minute College Plan Workout

1. Ellie Kay, "Q&A with Ellie Kay," *Life: Beautiful,* Spring 2010, 35.
2. www.collegeboard.com/prod_downloads/about/news_info/trends/trends_pricing_07.pdf.
3. "10 Alternative Ways to Cut College Costs," Bankrate.com, December 29, 2006, www.bankrate.com/brm/news/advice/college/oct06 cut college costs a2.asp.

Chapter 11: The 60-Minute Passion for a Home-Based Business Workout

1. "Half of U.S. Businesses Are Home-Based, Majority of Firms Self-Financed, Census Bureau Reports," U.S. Census Bureau, September 27, 2006, CB06-148, www.census.gov/newsroom/releases/archives/business_ownership/cb06-148.html.
2. "Advocacy Small Business Statistics and Research," U.S. Small Business Administration, web.sba.gov/faqs/faqIndexAll.cfm?areaid=24.

Chapter 12: The 60-Minute Launch Your Home-Based Business Workout

1. "Advocacy Small Business Statistics and Research," U.S. Small Business Administration, http://web.sba.gov/faqs/faqIndexAll.cfm?areaid=24.

Chapter 13: The 60-Minute Couple's Workout

1. Bill and Pam Farrel, *Men Are Like Waffles—Women Are Like Spaghetti* (Eugene, OR: Harvest House, 2007), 106–7.
2. Emerson Eggerichs, *Love and Respect: The Love She Most Desires, The Respect He Desperately Needs* (Nashville: Integrity, 2004), 11.

About the Author

Ellie Kay, known as America's Family Financial Expert®, is the best-selling author of fourteen books, including *Living Rich for Less* and *The Little Book of Big Savings*. She is a national television commentator for *Money Matters* and *Good Money* on ABC News NOW, a media veteran, a top-level international conference speaker, and a Fortune 500 corporate consumer consultant. Known for her dynamic personality and common sense strategies, Ellie is a frequent media guest on CNBC, CNN, and Fox. She is married to Bob Kay, a corporate pilot, and together they have seven children.

For more information about Ellie or about her financial help strategies, go to www.elliekay.com.

Want to be
Debt-free? Content? Generous?
Learn from America's Family Financial Expert®
and change the way you view money,
starting today!